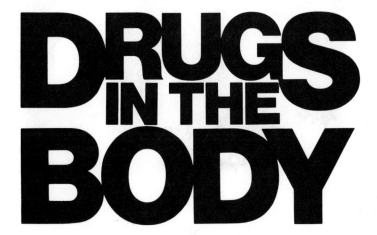

DRUGS
IN THE
BODY

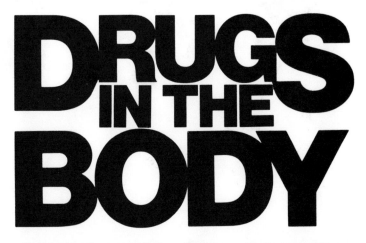

DRUGS IN THE BODY

EFFECTS OF ABUSE
BY MARK YOSLOW

FRANKLIN WATTS
NEW YORK/LONDON/TORONTO/SYDNEY

Photographs copyright ©: Photo Researchers Inc.: pp. 36 (Gregory G. Dimijian), 38 (Arthur Tress), 54 bottom (Richard Frear), 68 (Irene Vandermolen); Tony Freeman/PhotoEdit: p. 43 top; UPI/Bettmann Newsphotos: p. 43 bottom; Andrew Lichtenstein/Impact Visuals: p. 54 top; Comstock Photography Inc.: p. 73.

Library of Congress Cataloging-in-Publication Data

Yoslow, Mark.
    Drugs in the body / by Mark Yoslow.
      p. cm.
    Includes bibliographical references and index.
    Summary: Discusses the harmful effects of such drugs as cocaine, marijuana, psychedelic hallucinogens, and amphetamines.
    ISBN 0-531-12507-6
    1. Drugs—Physiological effect—Juvenile literature.   2. Drug abuse—Juvenile literature.   3. Psychotropic drugs—Physiological effect—Congresses.   [1. Drugs.   2. Drug abuse.]   I. Title.
RM301.17.Y67   1992
616.86—dc20   91-39030 CIP AC

CONTENTS

ACKNOWLEDGMENTS

My sincere appreciation goes to Dr. Charles Pippinger, one of the nation's leading experts in neuropharmacology, for the reference material he provided, and to Dr. Andrew Slaby for his expert review of this book.

To my wife, Robyn, thank you for dealing with the quibblings and scribblings of a writer.

To Tom Cohn for the clarity of his vision in defining the original topic, and to Lydia Stein for her consistent encouragement and worthwhile critique.

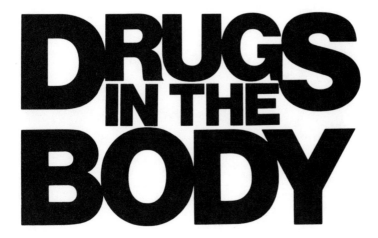

DRUGS IN THE BODY

1 ILLEGAL DRUGS AND BODY SYSTEMS

Brian's first class at high school is at 8:00. He lugs his books to the bus stop. He almost reaches it when he hears a familiar voice call out, "Hey, Brian. Hop in!" His friends Frank and Bobby are in Frank's new 4-wheeler. Brian jumps in the back seat. The marijuana smoke in the car is as thick as fog. Bobby chuckles a muffled hello between coughs.

"Something for the head?" Frank offers Brian the joint. Brian takes a long drag, coughs hard, rolls down the window, and spits out the phlegm in his mouth. He takes another long drag and passes the joint to Bobby, who comments, "So, you survived."

Frank is a drug dealer. Yesterday afternoon, he sold two grams of cocaine to Brian and Bobby. Their friend, Sharon, bought a gram of Ice (a smokable *amphetamine*) and a chunk of opiated hashish treated with *PCP*. Frank bought a six-pack of beer and a bottle of tequila for his regular customers. They had finished all of it among them. "Did you see how stoned Sharon was last night?" Frank laughs hard. "She was so gone, man. She loves speed and tequila."

"Yeah, I know," Brian replies. "Do you have any ups, man? I'm still wasted."

"Sure. I'll sell you five Black Beauties for only five bucks. Only because you're my pal." Frank is smiling. The small plastic bag is between the fingers of his right hand, which is extended, palm open. Brian reaches into his pocket. He has $15 left from the $120 he earned at the record store at the mall last weekend, and it's only Wednesday. He hands Frank the money and swallows three of the pills.

The day flies by. Brian is very talkative in all of his classes, but most of what he says doesn't make much sense. After school, he meets Frank, Bobby and Sharon, who is very high on Ice. Her hands are shaking as she nervously smokes a cigarette. Frank says he's received a delivery of blotter acid (LSD). Bobby has a bottle of vodka. Two hours later, Brian is in the park watching an ant making its way through the bark around the trunk of the tree. He sees the bark repeatedly melt and become solid. He follows the ant for what seems to be a few minutes. Four hours pass. Sharon chatters at Frank and Bobby about anything that comes into her head, and cannot concentrate on any subject for more than a few minutes.

Over the last few months, Brian has been spending more time and more money on staying high as much as possible. He has been allowing his body or his friends to decide the time of the day to take a *drug* and how much to take. But lately, he has had a deep congestion in his chest in the mornings. The phlegm he coughs up has spots of blood in it. He also wakes up with throbbing headaches, and takes large doses of aspirin to control them. If he bends over for a couple of minutes he gets nosebleeds. Slowly, all of these are getting worse. Aside from these discomforts, he has diarrhea minutes after he eats. His skin is cool and clammy, his hair dry and brittle. He does not know all of these signs are important. He is sixteen years old, does not think he is ill, and believes the coughing, bleeding and pain will "go away" as usual.

Brian is involved in something that is much harder to stop than it is to start. A small part of this problem is taking drugs and overcoming addiction. The larger, more important part is coping with the number of adverse emotional and physical effects these drugs are having on his body. He does not know that many of these effects will remain with him for the rest of his life.

He avoids his parents. He is afraid they will stop him from using marijuana, cocaine, amphetamines and alcohol. He tells himself he likes being high. He does not know he is addicted to all of these drugs at the same time. Hashish, a highly concentrated marijuana product, contains chemicals that cause *paranoia,* a deep form of fear. Other chemicals in marijuana cause *hallucinations:* the senses of sight, hearing and touch no longer function normally. (The LSD in the blotter acid he took causes hallucinations that are more powerful, and added confusion to his fear.) All marijuana products cause addiction, and Brian's addiction to opiated hashish is reinforced by *opium* (it is used to make *heroin*), which causes a more powerful addiction.

Sometimes the hashish Brian smokes is also treated with PCP, a drug that causes both paranoia and powerful anger. His lungs are inflamed, and his coughing is caused by the smoke from the hashish pipe, which is hotter than cigarette smoke and contains more than twice as many irritating chemicals. Snorting cocaine is breaking down the sensitive membranes of his nose. They will not grow back. As long as he continues to take aspirin in large doses they will not heal and will keep bleeding, an effect of aspirin overdose. Coming down from all these drugs at the same time, especially cocaine, depresses him. The alcohol he is drinking increases that depression. He takes amphetamines in the morning to overcome a drug/alcohol hangover. Brian is in trouble.

Illegal drugs can cripple a person emotionally, mentally, or physically, sometimes in seconds or minutes, sometimes in a few weeks or months. The damaging internal effects a drug has on the brain, lungs, heart, liver, and kidneys (see Figure 1) are not always immediately obvious to the user. These effects build up slowly, starting as a cough or a slight pain or an inability to remember simple things quickly. Harmful physical reactions, which become more intense with continued drug use, are long-term effects.

The external physical and emotional effects that take place shortly after the drug is taken and absorbed by the body are more obvious to the user. The mind and body are in a state of being "high," the reason why the user takes the drug. These external effects are short-term effects.

A dose is the amount of a drug a person takes at one time. This can be a lot (a high dose) or a little (a low dose). Even if illegal drugs are used in low doses, they can never be considered truly safe. Drugs such as crack (crack cocaine)[1] and PCP[2] can cause changes in brain tissue that are nearly irreversible after only one 60-second exposure. There are no instructions or Surgeon General's warnings on dosage and short- or long-term use included with a joint, a vial of crack, or a set of heroin works (a syringe or an eyedropper equipped with a needle).

Some illegal drugs can and will fatally poison the body suddenly if the dose is too high, or poison the body slowly if taken consistently over a long period of time.

None of this is obvious to someone under the influence of drugs. The effect the drug has on the mind can blind the user to the effect the drug is having on the body. The hard evidence of the long-term effects of illegal drugs can be seen as a gradual breakdown in the muscles and nerves of regular users and in the

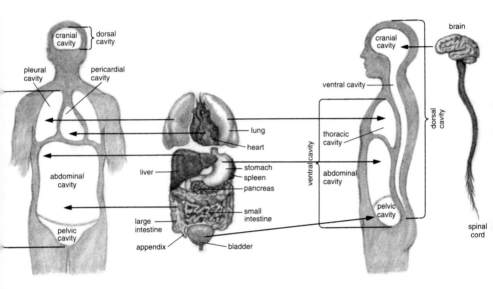

cranial cavity
dorsal cavity
pleural cavity
pericardial cavity

abdominal cavity
liver

pelvic cavity
large intestine
appendix

lung
heart
stomach
spleen
pancreas
small intestine
bladder

cranial cavity
ventral cavity
thoracic cavity
ventral cavity
abdominal cavity
pelvic cavity

dorsal cavity

brain
spinal cord

FIGURE 1: INTERNAL ORGANS OF THE BODY
Illegal drugs travel in the bloodstream and can affect
the functions of all internal organs in the body: the lungs,
heart, liver, pancreas, stomach, intestines, and kidneys.

ways body and mind work together after five or ten
years.

The amount of an addictive drug a user requires
always increases as time goes by. This is because the
mind and body develop a *tolerance* for the drug.[3]
This means that, after repeated exposure, body systems become accustomed to the drug's effect. As tolerance increases, the user must take *more* of the drug
and must take it *more often* to achieve its short-term
effect. Consistent use at higher and higher doses will
have the long-term effect of gradually breaking down
the emotions and thought processes that make up an

15

individual's personality. Eventually, some functions of the vital organs, such as the heart and lungs, may be affected as well.

Doctors cannot do anything for a user under the influence of an illegal drug until they know what drug the person has taken. Other drugs, called *antidotes,* that can stop the negative effects of a drug and save a person's life, cannot be given unless the substance has been identified. Doctors cannot do very much to help a person who is showing the psychological effects of an illegal drug if he or she cannot communicate. PCP, as well as some of the newer *"designer drugs,"* can block the area of the brain that controls speech.

EFFECTS ON BODY SYSTEMS[4]

Many drugs affect the entire body. A few, however, affect either the brain or the body. To reach the brain, a drug must enter the bloodstream (see Figure 2), which carries the substance throughout the body, whether it is swallowed, smoked, sniffed (snorted), or injected. The way a drug was originally made and the way it is taken will affect the time it takes to reach the brain. There are no hard and fast rules, though, to determine which method of taking a drug will cause it to reach the brain in the shortest period of time.

In most cases, smoking and inhaling will allow a drug to reach the brain in the shortest period of time. Microscopic blood vessels in the lungs, called capillaries, absorb oxygen and the vapors in the smoke that can dissolve in blood. This blood reaches the brain in about seven to eight seconds and then travels to the rest of the body.

Injection into a vein is the second fastest route to the brain and takes approximately one to two minutes, except in the case of PCP, which reaches the brain in only three to five seconds.

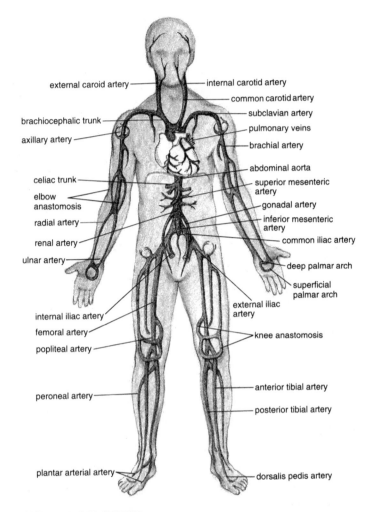

external caroid artery — — internal carotid artery

— common carotid artery

— subclavian artery

brachiocephalic trunk — — pulmonary veins

axillary artery — — brachial artery

— abdominal aorta

celiac trunk — — superior mesenteric artery

elbow anastomosis — — gonadal artery

radial artery — — inferior mesenteric artery

renal artery — — common iliac artery

ulnar artery — — deep palmar arch

— superficial palmar arch

internal iliac artery — external iliac artery

femoral artery — — knee anastomosis

popliteal artery —

— anterior tibial artery

peroneal artery — — posterior tibial artery

plantar arterial artery — — dorsalis pedis artery

FIGURE 2: BLOOD STREAM AND CIRCULATORY SYSTEM

This system consists of the heart, and all the vessels that travel between the heart and lungs, as well as between the heart and the rest of the body. Blood travels first from the heart to the lungs to pick up oxygen. Oxygen-rich blood returns to the heart, is pumped directly to the brain, and then travels throughout the body.

The third fastest route is grinding or chopping a drug into a very fine powder, then sniffing or snorting it. The powder sticks to the moist lining of the nose; capillaries in the nose carry the drug to the brain in about one to five minutes.

Usually, a drug will reach the brain very slowly if it is eaten, then absorbed through the walls of the stomach and small intestine. This can take anywhere from 20 minutes to one hour.

People who use illegal drugs want them to affect their brain. Even though some people will take certain ones to augment their sexual experiences or to speed up their muscular reaction times, the place drugs have the most powerful effect is the brain.

The Brain

The brain is the central location of messages that are received from and sent to the body. Every type of tissue, every organ, every muscle, nerve, and blood vessel, every aspect of personality and behavior is represented in the brain (see Figure 3). When illegal drugs enter the brain, they change the way it relates to other body systems and the way it uses and stores information. Drugs turn such complex tasks as driving a car or using a power tool into dangerous events. They alter the way the brain interprets sensations from the outside world.

At its highest level, the brain is a system that specializes in creative ideas and logical analyses. At its most basic, the brain focuses its creative and logical forces on survival.

The brain is the principal part of the *central nervous system* and is divided into distinct areas that control behavior and regulate the organ systems of the body. It receives information through the spinal cord and the *cranial* (skull) *nerves.* Starting from where the spinal cord enters the brain, the *medulla* controls *res-*

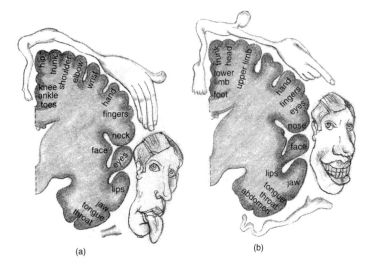

FIGURE 3: BODY FUNCTIONS AND THE AREAS OF THE BRAIN
The functions of every organ and muscle in the body are controlled
by a specific area of the brain. Illegal drugs chemically alter
messages traveling back and forth between the body and the
brain. While these drugs are in the body, brain functions are
impaired temporarily, or permanently if drug impurities cause
areas of the brain to die. The area of the brain represented here
is the size of a stack of five silver dollars. Shown are both motor
(a) and sensory (b) functions.

piration, blood pressure, and heart rate. The *reticular
formation* takes shape after the medulla, extends
through the *pons* (Latin for "bridge," because it joins
the spinal cord with the mass of the brain), and
spreads out to all the areas of the brain. The reticular
formation is responsible for normal wakefulness and
alertness. Next is the *cerebellum,* which controls
equilibrium, posture, and all muscular movements.

Between the cerebellum and the *cerebrum* is the
midbrain, which contains centers that communicate
pain and pleasure (see Figure 4). The *hypothalamus*
controls hunger, thirst, temperature, aggression, and
sex drive, and, by regulating the pituitary gland, con-

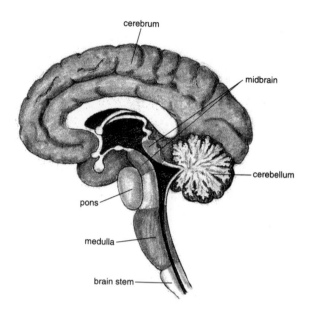

cerebrum

midbrain

cerebellum

pons

medulla

brain stem

FIGURE 4: THE CEREBRUM
This is the largest part of the human brain. It controls
our judgment, emotions, logic, and learning. It is the only
area of the brain that actually "thinks," and allows the
body to develop and refine complex muscular skills.

trols the secretion of many hormones. Nerve pathways that extend from the hypothalamus to the cerebrum influence the emotions, sleep, and wakefulness.
The *thalamus* is in charge of sensory transmission
(sight, hearing, touch, taste) and perception.

The cerebrum, the largest part of the human
brain, surrounds the midbrain. It is the center of
learning, memory, intelligence, reasoning, creative
thought, and imagination, as well as complex sensory
and motor activities, such as identifying the musical
sounds that form a symphony, making an architectural
drawing of a house, or dancing in a ballet.

Drugs and the Brain:
Psychological Aspects
The effect a drug has on the brain can be expressed as changes in the way an individual feels about himself and others. A person under the influence of an illegal drug can become emotionally violent. He or she can deeply hurt the feelings, and lose the trust, of parents, friends, spouse, and business associates.

It is difficult to see that using a drug is causing emotional changes in yourself. It is similar to getting dirt on your face and not knowing it until you notice your reflection in a mirror.

We use the brain to develop judgment, the ability to tell if something is present or absent, right or wrong, big or small. Most of the time, the brain can easily judge the condition of the body and tell if it is feeling healthy or ill. However, it is difficult for the brain to judge itself and see that it is emotionally healthy or ill. The brain normally operates in a positive manner. In a sense, it needs to believe what it thinks and must trust the sensations it receives from the body—what the body feels, hears, sees, and tastes.

When a drug alters the way the brain receives and uses information, the brain does not function in the same way it would if the user were straight. Something learned in school while a student is high, for example, may be remembered the next day as a confused jumble. A friend can suddenly seem like an enemy. An enemy can as easily become a friend. A gesture of friendship or affection can be seen as a violent attack.

At first, a user often finds it easy to identify differences in how he or she feels emotionally and physically when high as compared to being straight. The user is able to judge how high he or she will get with a certain amount of a drug. After using a drug several times a day, every day for a few weeks, though, a type of confusion in judgment begins. The user loses the ability to separate the feelings that are generated by a drug experience from real feelings. It is very difficult to see this happening in oneself. Close friends or professionals such as medical doctors or psychologists must, in most cases, tell the user that he or she is changing emotionally, as a result of using drugs.

Certain types of drugs will cause the user to "dissociate," a mental state in which only a part of the personality can function, making the user feel as though he or she is a different person with a different sense of right and wrong. In this mental state, the opportunity to cause injury to others seems free of punishment. The need for money or anything a user wants can overcome his or her ability to judge the difference between right and wrong.

Confusion, passive or aggressive behavior, and violent crime go hand in hand with use of illegal drugs.

The Lungs and the Respiratory System

When a user smokes an illegal drug to get high, his or her lungs become less able to absorb oxygen and transfer it to red blood cells (see Figure 5).

The lungs are lined with tiny air sacs, called *alveoli,* that are surrounded by capillaries. It is here that *respiration* takes place, which is the transfer of oxygen from the lungs to the bloodstream and carbon dioxide from the bloodstream to the lungs (see Figure 6).

When a drug is smoked and inhaled, the alveoli are coated with tars and resins—the sticky solid particles that make smoke look gray or brown—and there is a significant decrease in efficient respiration. Also, the types of compounds in smoke cause a number of

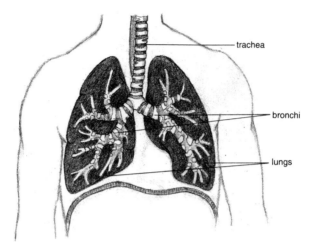

FIGURE 5: RESPIRATORY SYSTEM
The trachea is a tube-shaped structure made of rings of
cartilage lined with special cells, which leads to the bronchi,
the two branching "trees" that enter the lungs. The lobes
of the lungs are made up of branching sacs called the alveoli.

respiratory disorders, ranging from chronic *bronchitis*
to *pneumonia, emphysema,* and *lung cancer.*

Bronchitis is a serious infection caused by organisms entering and growing in the system of tubes that
conduct air into the lungs (see Figure 7). The system
begins with the *trachea* (or windpipe), located in the
neck. The trachea branches into two larger tubes, the
bronchi, which enter the lungs. Together they make
up the upper respiratory system. The bronchi are
lined with cells that have microscopic, muscular,
threadlike structures, called cilia, which beat in rhythmic waves to stop particles of dust from entering the
lungs. They are the first line of defense for the respiratory system (see Figure 8). When exposed to super-
heated air, tars, and resins, these cells die, and
organisms such as bacteria or viruses, which attach

23

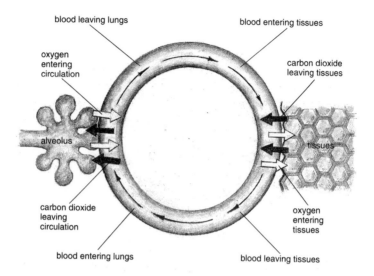

FIGURE 6: CYCLE OF RESPIRATION
The supply of oxygen to all the cells of the body, and the removal of carbon dioxide, depends upon the exchange of these gases by red blood cells (RBCs). When RBCs circulate through capillaries alongside cells in the body, they drop off oxygen and pick up carbon dioxide. Then the RBCs travel in the bloodstream to the lungs, where they pass through capillaries alongside the alveoli, drop off carbon dioxide, pick up oxygen, and the cycle begins again.

themselves to dust particles in the air, can enter the upper respiratory system and cause bronchitis.

Chronic bronchitis is a form of this infection that is recurring. The condition is very difficult to cure in smokers, and makes marijuana and crack users cough up mucus and residue from the smoke. Because the path to the lungs is no longer healthy, bacteria and viruses can travel deep into the lungs and cause infections there as well.

The smaller tubes that lead to the alveoli are called *bronchioles,* and together with the lobes of the

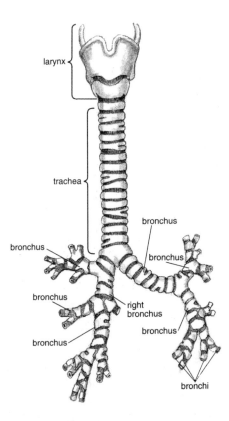

larynx

trachea

bronchus

bronchus

bronchus

bronchus

bronchus

right
bronchus

bronchus

bronchus

bronchi

**FIGURE 7: UPPER RESPIRATORY
SYSTEM: TRACHEA AND BRONCHI**
These structures are lined with moist, protective tissues,
which are destroyed by smoking. The resulting dead and dying
cells become a feeding and breeding ground for organisms
that cause respiratory infections.

lungs are referred to as the lower respiratory system
(see Figure 9). When the alveoli become irritated or
inflamed by the hot smoke from crack or marijuana,
they are more susceptible to infections and chronic
diseases.

People who develop pneumonia, an infection in
which the lungs fill with fluid, often need to be hospi-

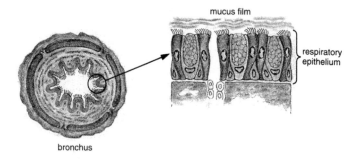

mucus film

respiratory
epithelium

bronchus

FIGURE 8: CILIATED RESPIRATORY EPITHELIUM
A layer of cells with threadlike cilia that continuously
sweep foreign particles and organisms back up the bronchi
and prevent them from entering the lungs. These cells are
bathed in a layer of mucus that their cilia keep moving
away from the lungs. The mucus is coughed out.

talized. Their breathing becomes so impaired that
they are provided with an oxygen mask. As the infection is controlled by antibiotics, the fluid that has col-
lected in the lungs is slowly absorbed by the blood
vessels surrounding the alveoli.

In emphysema, a chronic lung disorder directly
associated with smoking, the alveoli fill with fluid and
stretch, creating deep pockets where more fluid col-
lects. This causes shallow breathing and a constant,
wet cough. People who have emphysema feel as if
they are drowning. Currently, there is no cure.

The most deadly disease of the respiratory system
is lung cancer. Cells in the lung stop growing normally,
multiply very rapidly, and no longer carry out the
process of breathing. No one is certain of the causes
of cancer; however, there is more lung cancer among
people who smoke than among those who do not.

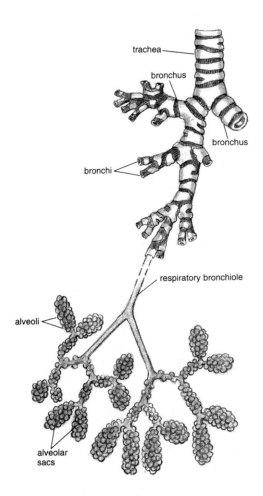

trachea

bronchus

bronchus

bronchi

respiratory bronchiole

alveoli

alveolar
sacs

**FIGURE 9: LOWER RESPIRATORY SYSTEM:
BRONCHIOLES AND ALVEOLI**
Smaller forms of the bronchi gradually decrease in size as
they reach the groups of cells that shape the alveoli.

There is a great deal of evidence suggesting that compounds in the tars and resins of smoke may react with the genes in lung cells and cause mutations in cells that can become cancerous.

The Heart

Some drugs have a strong negative effect on the cells that make up heart muscle or on the nerves that keep the heart beating (see Figure 10). The speed of a beating heart is measured in the number of beats per minute and is called the heart rate. Some drugs speed up the heart rate; others slow it down. Still others may cause cardiac arrest, in which case the heart can permanently stop.

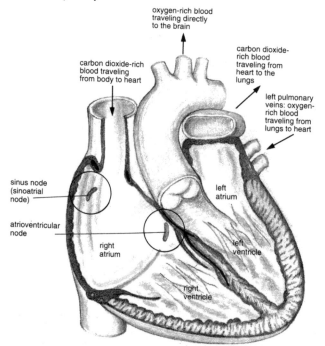

FIGURE 10: NERVES THAT KEEP THE HEART BEATING
These nerves are actually two bundles of concentrated, special fibers called nodes. The first bundle, the sinoatrial (SA) node, makes the heart pump carbon dioxide-rich blood coming from the body into the lungs where RBCs exchange this gas for oxygen. The SA node is the pacemaker of the heart because it stimulates the second bundle of fibers, the atrioventricular (AV) node. The AV node makes the heart pump oxygen-rich blood, coming from the lungs, back to the brain and body.

A faster heart rate requires more oxygen. Respiration, the process whereby all tissues take in oxygen and release carbon dioxide, increases. The lungs expand and contract faster to meet the demands of heart muscle and all the other muscles of the body.

Some drugs can cause *tachycardia,* a fluttering of the heart. A heart that beats much faster than normal for long periods of time can develop very small rips in its muscular walls. These heal and form scars that do not stretch the same way as healthy muscle tissue, and sometimes will not stretch at all. A heart like this can no longer pump the same amount of blood. The young person with a heart that is damaged in this way may feel as tired as an elderly man or woman.

The Liver

The most dangerous drugs have a powerful effect on the liver, the chemical plant of the body (see Figure 11). The liver is made up of millions of small bundles of cells surrounded by capillaries (see Figure 12). These cells have six major functions[5] that are essential to life:

1. Production of bile (sent to the small intestine to help digest fats).
2. Fuel separation (glucose) and storage (as *glycogen*).
3. Production of blood-clotting factors (used by the blood to stop cuts from bleeding and to form scabs).
4. Production of plasma proteins (used by the immune system to defend and maintain the body).
5. Formation of urea from ammonia (a poison produced by cells after the breakdown of protein).
6. Removal of chemical waste from the body (included in bile).

The liver is responsible for making many molecules that are used in every organ and body process.

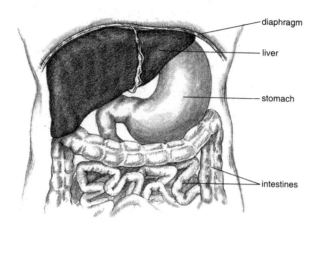

diaphragm

liver

stomach

intestines

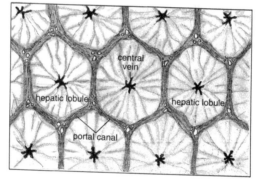

central vein

hepatic lobule

hepatic lobule

portal canal

FIGURE 11: THE LIVER

This organ has a spongy appearance because it is made up of millions of microscopic, circular structures, called *lobules*, that are surrounded and separated by capillaries. Each lobule has radial canals, like the spokes of a wheel, that travel toward its center. The canals collect energy-rich molecules and poisonous wastes from the bloodstream, and conduct them to groups of cells, with specialized functions, that line the walls of each canal.

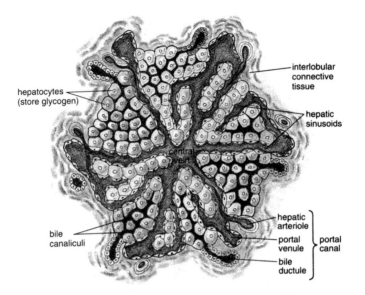

Labels on figure:
hepatocytes (store glycogen)

interlobular connective tissue

hepatic sinusoids

central vein

bile canaliculi

hepatic arteriole
portal venule
bile ductule
portal canal

FIGURE 12: CELLS IN THE LOBULES OF THE LIVER
Some cells along the canals of each lobule link small
molecules of sugar from digested food into long chains of
glycogen, the refined fuel used by all the tissues in the
body to create energy, and nearly all of it is made and
prepared for storage by these cells. Other cells convert
waste products into non-poisonous compounds (bile and urea)
for removal from the body. Still others produce complex
molecules used by blood and immune system cells.

It supplies fuel molecules every time the body springs
into action, especially for activities that require bursts
of energy, such as lifting a heavy weight, or making a
leap in ballet, or catching a ball. It also supplies the
brain with fuel that powers the ability to think.

The liver links short molecules of glucose, a sugar,
into long chains, called glycogen, which are stored as
a reserve fuel supply in the liver and muscles. Glycogen is made out of sugars from the digestion of carbo-

hydrate foods. When the buildup of glycogen reserves is satisfied, any remaining sugars are converted to fat and stored in fat cells beneath the skin. When fuel is needed by the body during normal daily activities and for sudden bursts of energy, enzymes from the liver break down glycogen into glucose. However, these reserves can be depleted by continuous physical activity over a period of time greater than 15 minutes, such as running fast for a long distance. When the muscles demand more fuel for endurance, the liver produces enzymes that convert the fat molecules stored in fat cells into glucose.

In addition, the liver separates molecules from the blood that it identifies as wastes, impurities, or poisons and chemically changes them into safer molecules that will not hurt the body. It sends some of these molecules along with bile into the gall bladder, through the intestines, and out of the body. Through

FIGURE 13: THE KIDNEYS (TOP)
These organs receive blood that has traveled throughout the body carrying wastes produced by cells, especially urea from the liver. Made of bundles of thin tubes, they perform two functions on blood *serum*, the fluid in blood. (1) They separate blood cells from serum and return these cells to the bloodstream. (2) Then they remove wastes, urea, and some water from serum, which is sent to the bladder as urine, and return the clean serum to circulation.

FIGURE 14: THE GLOMERULUS (BOTTOM)
The microscopic structure where serum is separated from the cells in blood, starting the process of cleaning the body's fluids.

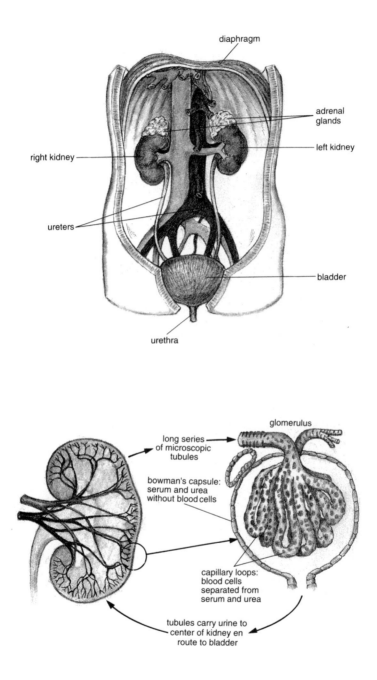

diaphragm

adrenal glands

right kidney

left kidney

ureters

bladder

urethra

glomerulus

long series of microscopic tubules

bowman's capsule: serum and urea without blood cells

capillary loops: blood cells separated from serum and urea

tubules carry urine to center of kidney en route to bladder

its capillaries, the liver removes ammonia and converts it into urea, which is released into the bloodstream and travels to the kidneys.

Chemical fragments of an illegal drug or an impurity in the drug can become trapped in the liver cells. If these build up, they can become a slow-acting poison in the liver and interrupt the balance of the body's chemical reactions. Drug impurities may also damage the genes in liver cells and cause cancer or tumors.

The Kidneys

These are the final filters that produce urine (see Figure 13). The kidneys are made of millions of capillaries linked to specialized structures, called *glomeruli*, which act as microscopic sewer grates (see Figure 14). They are designed to separate those molecules that are to be returned to the bloodstream from urea molecules that are to be removed from the body. The urea is converted to urine and sent to the bladder, where it is excreted.

2 COCAINE AND CRACK

Cocaine may be the most dangerous illegal drug ever introduced in the United States, not only because of its short- and long-term effects on the mind and body, but because of the crime that surrounds the drug. Cocaine is so addictive, especially in the form of crack, that the demand is overwhelming. Instead of realizing how dangerous the drug is, many people erroneously believe it can be used for recreation.

HISTORY AND COUNTRIES OF ORIGIN[1]

Cocaine is made from the leaves of the *coca* plant, which grows wild in South America. "Coca" comes from *kúka,* a word from the Quechan peoples, the ancient Indians of Peru.

The most famous civilization among the Quechan peoples was the Inca, an Indian race noted for its fully developed culture that included artists, merchants, craftsmen, and priests who were the leaders of a complex religion with many gods. The culture flourished more than 500 years ago, but the only evidence of its existence are ruins of vast cities complete with areas of government, commerce, and science.

The coca plant, Erythroxylon coca.
Cocaine is produced from its leaves.

The *stimulant* effects of cocaine were discovered long before its use in Europe and North America by the Inca and other South American peoples. The Inca priests believed that the trancelike state induced by chewing the leaves of the coca plant permitted more direct communication with the gods, whose demands were interpreted from signs and symbols in the natural environment.

Cocaine, the intoxicating ingredient in coca leaves, is an *alkaloid,* a naturally occurring substance that comes from plants. In its natural form it will not dissolve in water. A drug will be more readily absorbed by the body if it can dissolve in water, that is, if it is soluble in water. When coca leaves are chewed, the juice is partially digested by hydrochloric acid in the stomach. Cocaine reacts with hydrochloric acid to become cocaine hydrochloride, which is soluble in water. In the laboratory, solutions can be made of cocaine hydrochloride for medicinal purposes.

Cocaine acts as an *anesthetic.* When it is placed on the moist tissues of the eyes, nose, or mouth, it makes the nerves in these areas become numb. When taken internally in larger doses, however, cocaine has the opposite effect: it acts as a stimulant.

The Spanish explorers of South America wrote about how the Indians of Peru could sustain hard labor for much longer periods of time when they chewed the leaves of the coca plant. These explorers brought samples of the plant to Europe in the late sixteenth century.

About two hundred years later, cocaine found extraordinary usefulness in medicine as a *local anesthetic,* a drug that is used to make a small area of the body numb to pain. In Germany, in 1884, it was used by Dr. Karl Koller for the first time in eye surgery. Before the use of cocaine, this surgery was difficult to perform because it was extremely painful. It was also during this year that cocaine became known as a won-

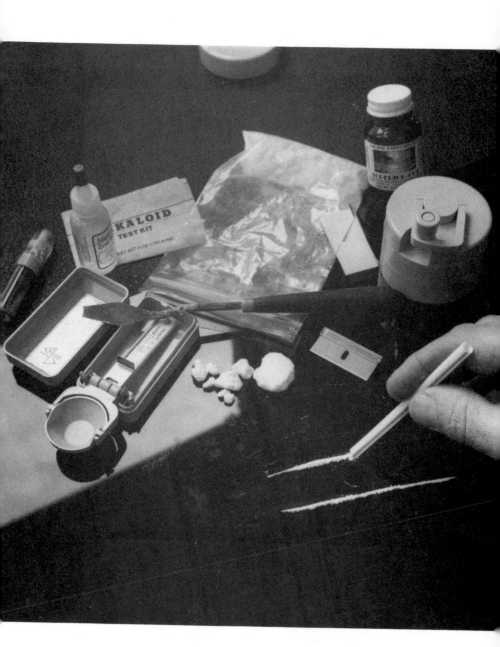

Paraphernalia of cocaine use.
Cocaine is often "snorted" through a tube.

der drug. Papers were written about it by many doctors, including Sigmund Freud, the father of modern psychoanalysis. But cocaine was already being used in other ways that had little to do with medicine.

Twenty years earlier, in 1863, Angelo Mariani, a chemist from Corsica, created a mixture of coca extract and wine that he called Vin Mariani. It became one of the most popular medical elixirs of the age and made its inventor wealthy. In the late nineteenth century, an elixir was a type of home remedy that people would drink. There were many elixirs available that were supposed to stop baldness, make old people young, or cure colds overnight. Very few of these were able to provide the results the makers promised. However, because Vin Mariani contained enough cocaine to be a stimulant, it made people feel very energetic.[2]

Following Mariani's preparation, cocaine was used as a stimulant in a variety of products by Europeans and Americans until the 1920s. This continued interest in cocaine was supported by scientific and medical papers that called it a wonder drug in 1884. For example, in 1885 in Atlanta, Georgia, a pharmacist named John Styth Pemberton invented a drink he called "French Wine of Coca, Ideal Tonic," presumably as an American elixir to replace Vin Mariani. This drink did not become as popular as Vin Mariani, as Pemberton hoped it would, so in 1886 he removed the alcohol, added kola nut extract and citrus oils, and renamed the drink Coca-Cola.

Pemberton sold Coca-Cola as a medicine, a headache remedy, and a stimulant. In 1888 he began using soda water, instead of noncarbonated water, to make his beverage.

In 1891 Asa Griggs Chandler, another pharmacist, bought the right to manufacture Coca-Cola and started the Coca-Cola Company the following year.

This company and its product are the reason why the corner drugstore in the United States has a soda fountain: Coca-Cola was dispensed for a few pennies at the counter. The drink soon became extremely popular across the United States. When the early advertisements for Coca-Cola said the drink gave people a lift, they meant it.

At the turn of the century, when the addictive properties of cocaine were identified, legislation was passed to limit the sale and use of the drug. The Pure Food and Drug Act of 1906 included cocaine in its list of substances that could not be sold without medical approval. Before 1906, executives at the Coca-Cola Company had cocaine removed from its formula. They realized that cocaine addiction was becoming a public concern and did not want the soft drink associated with abuse of the drug. Yet even in 1909, sixty-nine imitations of Coca-Cola that contained cocaine were still available in drug stores.

With the advent of new technology in the field of drug manufacturing, from the 1920s to today, synthetic drugs related to cocaine were developed that proved to be more effective as local anesthetics. Such drugs as novocaine, procaine, lidocaine, and benzocaine are still used in surgery on the eye, the skin (dermatology), and in dentistry to make external or internal tissues numb to pain.

The cocaine that is obtained today for recreational use has changed from that available in the 1920s. Most of the white powder manufactured by illegal laboratories and sold as cocaine actually contains anywhere from 25 percent to 65 percent of the drug in its pure form. However, at the dealer and pusher level of the cocaine trade, the product sold may contain very little if any cocaine.

Some of the drugs used by dealers to dilute or "cut" cocaine are synthetic local anesthetics.[3] Stimulants such as caffeine and amphetamines ("speed") are also used. Many dealers add phencyclidine (PCP) to cocaine. PCP is a central nervous system depressant. When it was first developed, it was used to keep laboratory animals docile and quiet during experiments. Because it was so effective in animals, it was recommended for use as an anesthetic in humans. Its use in humans was discontinued because it caused people to have rages and behave violently. Legally, PCP is only allowed to be used in laboratory animals. Illegally, it is used to cut cocaine. Combinations of all of these drugs produce an effect that is very similar to the one caused by cocaine in the user's body and brain, even though the white, flaky powder will not contain any cocaine.

The purer forms of cocaine sold on the street are usually diluted with sugars and sugar derivatives such as glucose, lactose, *mannitol,* and inositol.

"Rock cocaine" describes a mixture of cocaine and baking soda or sodium bicarbonate. Another name for rock cocaine is crack.

HOW COCAINE IS USED

Cocaine can be used in any of three ways. It can be sniffed (snorted) from a small spoon, spatula, or long fingernail. It can also be sniffed through a metal or glass tube after the drug has been formed into a "line" on a piece of glass or mirror. This is the most popular method of using the drug. Cocaine can be "cooked" or heated with water and injected into a vein. It can also be smoked.

The original method of smoking cocaine was to mix the drug with ether and ignite it in a pipe. This method is called freebasing. Ether is a flammable, volatile, explosive liquid that burns at a very low temperature. Its vapors will ignite in air if they are exposed to a spark. The actor Richard Pryor was badly burned when the vapors near a bottle of ether that he was using to freebase cocaine accidentally ignited. The bottle exploded in his face when he struck a match to light a cigarette. The smoke that is created by cocaine is extremely high in temperature and kills the ciliated cells lining the bronchi and bronchioles in the lungs.

The new method of smoking cocaine is to first make it into rock cocaine or crack, place it in the bowl of a water pipe, then ignite it. This mixture creates smoke that is higher in temperature, even if a water pipe is used to bubble the smoke through water and cool it down. Crack smoke also destroys the protective cells in the upper respiratory system.

Very little cocaine is required to make a large quantity of crack. For this reason, it is very inexpensive and has become the preferred way of selling cocaine on the street, since the addiction is stronger and the profits are much higher.

COCAINE, CRACK, AND THE BODY[4, 5]

There are many variables that affect the way cocaine is absorbed and *metabolized,* or broken down by the body. Different people will require different doses of the drug to feel its effects whether it is smoked, injected, or sniffed.

Cocaine creates a state of mind called *euphoria,* an exaggerated feeling of physical and emotional well-being. When users smoke crack cocaine, the drug takes effect faster and with greater intensity than when it is injected or sniffed. The length of time it takes for the drug to take effect depends on how long it takes for enough molecules of cocaine to enter the brain.

Cocaine is an addictive drug: *addicts* need to keep taking it to stop *withdrawal* feelings from occurring.

(Above) Crack is a smokable form of cocaine.
(Below) A crack pipe

A person will become addicted to the drug if it is used repeatedly because it stops the brain from carrying out an important chemical reaction involving a compound called *dopamine.*

The human brain produces dopamine in response to pleasurable experiences. This chemical is produced whenever an individual feels, smells, sees, or tastes something he or she enjoys. Normally, dopamine is released by special cells in the brain for a short period of time, from a few seconds to a few minutes. Then, other cells start absorbing the dopamine for recycling, and the pleasurable experience becomes less intense until it passes. Cocaine prevents these cells from absorbing and recycling the dopamine. Crack cocaine stops this reaction much faster, and can cause a sudden, powerful addiction after a single use.

When cocaine is sniffed or injected, the blocking of dopamine absorption occurs gradually, which keeps the brain mildly stimulated, and passes slowly. However, when crack is smoked, there is a massive blocking of dopamine absorption that is very sudden. Stimulation of the brain is very intense, and lasts for 15 minutes—the length of the crack high. In crack cocaine addiction, the addict is controlled by the brain's demand for exposure to dopamine.

From the First 8 Seconds
to the First 30 Minutes

The peak effect of cocaine when it is sniffed occurs in about 30 minutes. The peak effect when the drug is injected into a vein occurs in about a minute. However, the peak effect of crack, or rock cocaine, when it is smoked occurs in 8 seconds, or the time it takes blood to circulate from the lungs to the brain.

There is one area of the brain where the blocking of dopamine absorption is very important, and that is the pleasure/pain center, located in the hypothalamus, an area shared by the midbrain and the cerebrum (see Figure 15). When an addict knows he or she is going to get some cocaine, dopamine will be released in the pleasure/pain center, where it stimulates the nerve endings in anticipation of satisfying the need for the drug. As soon as the drug reaches the hypothalamus, the brain is bathed in dopamine. The reason why crack addicts smoke the drug as often as they can is because the nerve endings in the pleasure center are exposed to dopamine for 15 minutes, a period hundreds of times longer than the normal few seconds. The drive for crack created by this reaction in the brain can overcome every other drive or thought in the mind of the crack cocaine addict, and can cause people to become addicted after smoking it only once.

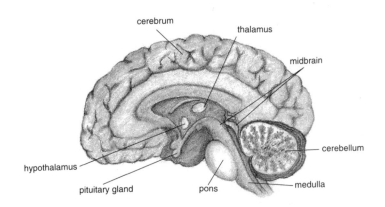

FIGURE 15: THE HYPOTHALAMUS
Located near the base of the brain, this structure informs the brain of specific needs that must be met, such as hunger, thirst, proper temperature, and sexual fulfillment. As one of the most important pleasure centers of the brain, it is very sensitive to the neurotransmitter dopamine.

From the First Day
to the First Month

After a few weeks of cocaine use, the brain cells that normally produce dopamine become exhausted. At the same time, the brain cells that normally absorb dopamine become so accustomed to being blocked that they develop a condition called chronic reuptake blockade: they stop absorbing dopamine on their own, even when cocaine is not in the brain. This increases the already powerful craving for the drug.

Normally, we have cravings for water, food, and procreation that are part of the basic survival drives that keep us alive. These drives are controlled by areas in the brain that produce, release, and absorb dopamine. Cocaine tricks these areas of the brain and creates a drive that identifies the drug as necessary for survival. The craving for cocaine in an addict becomes as powerful as the cravings for food and water in a person who is starving and dehydrated.

The dopamine in a normal brain is absorbed and recycled for use many times. In a cocaine addict's brain the cells that produce dopamine in the pleasure center are so exhausted that other areas of the brain will start manufacturing dopamine to compensate for the loss.

Cocaine addiction also has a psychological side effect called cocaine *dysphoria,* a feeling of impatience and restlessness combined with the feeling of sadness or anger. Such feelings can occupy the mind of an addict when he or she runs out of the drug. Cocaine dysphoria is at the root of crimes committed by cocaine addicts.

From the First Month
to the First Year

The smoke from a crack pipe has a very high temperature that scientists refer to as superheated air. When the moist tissues of the lungs are exposed to super-heated air the first time crack is smoked, some of the cells lining the upper respiratory system are killed within seconds. Many of them die if the drug is smoked repeatedly over a period of hours. A very large number will die if crack is smoked over a period of days, weeks, or months. The protection these cells provide the lungs is gradually removed during the first few days or weeks, depending upon the original condition of the crack smoker's lungs. Once the defense system of the lungs is broken down, pneumonia, emphysema, and chronic infections can develop.

If a user injects cocaine, he or she runs the risk of being infected with a number of different deadly diseases. The same way that crack smokers will share a pipe, intravenous (IV) cocaine users often share their needles. If one of the users is infected, the virus will be passed along to other users via the dirty needle. One of the viruses that is spread this way is the human immunodeficiency virus (HIV), which causes *acquired immune deficiency syndrome* (AIDS). The effects of this virus on the body can develop anywhere from a few months to ten years after exposure, depending upon the health of the person when first infected. When HIV disease progresses to AIDS, the body loses most of its ability to defend itself against illness.

There are many other diseases that can be passed along with a shared needle. *Hepatitis* is a viral infection that destroys the liver. *Endocarditis* is an infection of the tissue that surrounds the heart. *Meningitis* is an infection of the tissue that surrounds the brain, the source of the nerves for the entire body. If left untreated, and sometimes even with treatment, these diseases can kill those who are infected.

Users who sniff or snort cocaine develop different infections. The drug is pulled into the sinuses behind the nose with air and dust that carry many different types of bacteria and viruses. These organisms cause infections of the nose, or *rhinitis*. They also cause infections of the sinuses, or *sinusitis*.

Cocaine is a very harsh, caustic substance. It burns and breaks down the moist layer of skin inside the nose. It also causes the blood vessels inside the nose to contract very tightly. This keeps blood from circulating to these tissues to heal them. The combination of tissue breakdown and blood vessel contraction can cause the formation of holes in the tissue that divides the two passages of the nose. These holes rarely heal completely and can cause frequent nosebleeds. In many cases the nose changes shape after the cartilage that supports the nose has broken down. This can only be repaired with plastic surgery. However, the surgery is not possible unless there is enough tissue and cartilage remaining to permit a surgeon to rebuild the nose.

People who use cocaine "now and then" among their friends may not immediately develop the psychological and physical symptoms associated with the drug, and may not show any signs of cocaine addiction. Instead they may develop milder forms of these infections, and will probably experience cocaine dysphoria and depression for a few days. Recreational users, if they take cocaine as consistently as once a week to once a month, depending upon their physical and emotional condition, will accumulate the effects of the drug that are related to cocaine addiction, but over a much longer period of time.

Causes of Death

Unlike some other drugs, such as amphetamines ("speed"), cocaine does not need to be used repeatedly to cause seizures. A seizure is a short circuit in the brain that causes physical reactions similar to those of a person who has epilepsy. This involves loss of the ability to think or reason, loss of consciousness, loss of arm and leg coordination, and bladder and bowel control. This type of seizure may also be related to a *brain hemorrhage*, the bursting of a blood vessel.

Most people who use cocaine for the first time do not develop seizures. Depending upon the way they take the drug, the seizures usually start after they have become addicted and are taking larger doses. The process of addiction will take place over a period of days, weeks, or months. As the depletion of dopamine and the blocking of dopamine absorption increase, an addict will develop a higher tolerance for cocaine and use more of the drug more often.

Most cocaine addicts die of causes related to use of the drug. In this group, some will die of heart attacks, others will develop an infection of the nervous system. IV cocaine users, if they are not infected by HIV and develop AIDS, may develop bacterial infection of the bloodstream. IV cocaine users who inject an amount of the drug that has been mixed with benzocaine may develop blood clots. These can become trapped in the smaller vessels of the heart or the brain and cause a heart attack or stroke. Still other users will die of blockage of the kidneys. Many will die of respiratory failure if they take too much cocaine, because high doses chemically block the nerves that tell the lungs to keep breathing.

Cocaine dysphoria can lead to a deep *depression*. Users believe there is no way out of feeling so terrible, both physically and emotionally. If they do not seek out some form of psychological assistance and do not work at overcoming their depression, these people are liable to commit suicide.

3 OPIUM, MORPHINE, AND HEROIN

In many parts of the world, fields of poppies wave in the breeze. The color of the flowers, a rich red, is captivating. It is difficult to believe that something so beautiful could carry a curse of global magnitude. The most powerful forces in the illegal drug empires around the world can be found among the people who control the production of opium, morphine, and heroin, products of the poppy that cause strong addictions.

HISTORY AND COUNTRIES OF ORIGIN[1,2]

The opium poppy has a history that is thousands of years old. Opium as a drug has been in use in Eastern Europe, the Middle East, the Near East, and the Far East as a remedy and a form of escape for at least 2,500 years. In southwest Asia, the poppy is cultivated in Turkey, Afghanistan, Pakistan, and Iran, an area known as the Golden Crescent. In southeast Asia it is grown in Burma, Laos, and Thailand, an area known as the Golden Triangle. In the Western Hemisphere it is grown in Mexico and South America.

The methods of processing the poppy are as ancient as its use. No modern laboratories are necessary to obtain its basic products. The residue of the opium poppy's unripe seedpods, a milky white juice, is dried on a surface until it turns into a gooey brown gum. The gum is scraped and boiled, which hardens it to the consistency of soft, sticky rubber. This is rolled into balls or pressed into bricks and sold. *Morphine*, a drug named for Morpheus, the Greek god of dreams, is extracted or separated from opium. Through a simple chemical process, morphine can be converted to heroin.

All three of these drugs are *narcotic analgesics.* A narcotic is a stupor-producing drug. An analgesic is a drug that stops pain. All drugs that have opium as their original source are called opiates.

Unlike aspirin, which stops pain and usually does not affect the ability to remain attentive, narcotic analgesics put the user in a sleeplike state. People who are addicted to narcotics refer to this as "nodding out" when the drug reaches its peak effects. Actually, the user is neither asleep nor awake, but in a level of consciousness somewhere in between.

Opium had been popular in England for nearly a century before it was first introduced in the United States. In both countries, opium dens became popular, where for just a few pennies, a user would be provided with a pipe filled with raw opium and a cot. There the user would experience the drug's sleeplike effects. Opium was brought to the United States by the Chinese workers who built the railroads in the mid-1800s. Physicians and drug-manufacturing companies became aware of its medicinal properties, and opium was offered in a number of different tonics and tablets for everything from sour stomach to coughs and backaches.

Before opium was added to elixirs and home remedies in the United States, morphine was already being used for the same purposes throughout Europe and North America. Morphine was developed in Germany in 1805 and was promptly added to a number of products available in drug stores and grocery stores in the United States long before its addictive properties were fully understood.

In 1850 the injection syringe was invented, allowing for the easy administration of morphine and other drugs. Morphine's powerful painkilling properties were put to work during the Civil War in the United States, from 1861 to 1865. The first population of morphine addicts in the United States came out of that conflict.

In 1897 heroin was introduced as a "harmless" morphine substitute. The nightmare of addiction was going to be conquered by this new form of opiate. Morphine was replaced by heroin in the elixirs, tonics, and popular medicines of the day.

Ironically, heroin is three times more addictive than morphine; that is, only one third as many exposures to heroin can cause addiction, and morphine is less addictive than its parent drug, opium. Of these three highly addictive drugs, morphine is the least dangerous and is the only one used by doctors to ease certain types of extreme pain.

In 1914 the Harrison Act was passed, which required all manufacturers using opiates in any form to apply for a license to do so and to register for a tax on the drugs. By 1924 all heroin manufacture was outlawed in the continental United States, and the black market for the drug grew rapidly.

There have been several attempts to deal with heroin addiction on a large scale. There are still *methadone* clinics throughout the major cities of the United States. Methadone is the legal substitute for heroin. It is a longer acting and less expensive opiate.

However, as with heroin, withdrawal from methadone is prolonged, difficult, and fraught with depression caused by the drug's effect on areas of the brain that control moods.

HOW THE OPIATES
ARE USED

Opium can be placed in a pipe and smoked. This is done by heating the opium but not permitting it to burn. Heated opium gives off a yellowish vapor. Burning opium destroys most of its potent qualities. Cigarettes can be dipped in *paregoric,* a solution of opium mixed with camphor, and smoked. (Camphor is the compound used in mothballs.) Opium can also be prepared as a solution and swallowed.

Morphine is a brownish-white to white powder that can be smoked, made into tablets or a solution and swallowed, or injected into a muscle or just below the skin. The medicinal use of purified, pharmaceutically controlled morphine has a long history in the United States. It is safe to say that during the past fifty years, the number of morphine addicts created by the medical use of this analgesic is practically zero.

Heroin is a brown, tan, or white powder that can be smoked, snorted, swallowed, or injected. It is rarely effective for addicted users in any form other than a solution that is injected either intravenously or just below the skin.

Heroin and morphine in their powdered forms are weak bases, which makes it difficult for them to pass through the stomach wall. Drugs that are acidic are more quickly absorbed by the stomach. Swallowing heroin (or morphine) means having to wait more than an hour for the drug to take effect. Using the drug this way is considered a waste by addicts;

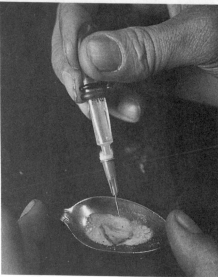

(Top) Drug addict and
his set of "works,"
including a bleach kit and
clean needle, which he
uses to inject a mixture
of cocaine and heroin.
(Left) How a "fix" of
heroin is prepared.
The drug is melted on a
spoon; it then may be drawn
through cotton in order
to strain out impurities.

injection is the preferred method.[3] The heroin user will begin with doses of 2 to 8 mg. Addicts will use as much as 450 mg per day.

Heroin addicts refer to intravenous injection as "mainlining" and to injection just below the skin as "skin popping." The solution for injection is prepared by dissolving the powder in a little bit of water held in a teaspoon. This is heated, or "cooked," with a match until it dissolves. A belt, piece of rubber tubing, rope, or heavy string is wound tightly around the arm to cause a vein to swell. The solution is drawn from the spoon into a syringe or eyedropper through a needle. The needle is inserted into a vein. Blood is drawn into the syringe and mixed with the solution. The solution and blood mixture is then injected into the vein.

Heroin can be cut, or diluted, with a number of different compounds that have the appearance of a white powder. This can be sugar, talcum powder, Epsom salts, mannitol, soap powder, or *quinine. Strychnine,* a deadly poison that, in very small doses, will cause mild tachycardia (rapidly beating heart), has also been used. A slightly greater dose of strychnine can cause convulsions. A moderate dose can cause death in a matter of minutes.

As with cocaine, a heroin addict will use *more* of the drug *more often* as the body develops tolerance. However, heroin is chemically different from cocaine, and its addiction is far more powerful once it is established. A very potent, addictive combination of heroin and cocaine known as *speedballs* caused the death of comedian John Belushi.

HEROIN AND
THE BODY[4]

Whenever you stub your toe, do you notice how the pain goes away after a few seconds? Granted, if you hurt yourself severely, the toe may be sore for days afterward. But the initial pain seems to go away pretty quickly. The reason is the action of a group of chemicals produced in the center of the brain, near the brain stem, called the *endorphins.*

As scientists researched the secret of opiate addiction and the areas of the brain that communicate feelings of pain and relief, they began to unravel the mystery of brain chemistry. They found that the endorphins play a key role in communicating pain and relief in the center of the brain, where the cerebrum, the midbrain, and the brain stem converge. They also found that the endorphins, the body's natural painkillers, can be replaced by heroin in the cerebrum and midbrain of the heroin addict.[5]

The midbrain is surrounded by the large mass of the cerebrum and is located just above the brain stem, the part of the brain that connects with the spinal cord (see Figure 16). These areas of the brain are considered primitive because they control aspects of survival and deep physical needs, such as the decrease of pain and the experience of pleasure. Structures shared by the midbrain and the cerebrum include the hypothalamus, the thalamus, and the *locus ceruleus.* The locus ceruleus is the most important area of the midbrain in addiction. It is here that the endorphins are replaced by opium, morphine, or heroin.

The endorphins were discovered during experiments in the 1970s that were designed to reveal the secret of addiction. Scientists found that these molecules, originally called *opioids,* attached themselves to the surfaces of brain cells in the locus ceruleus in the same positions as molecules of morphine and heroin. Both the opiate drug and endorphin molecules acted in a way that was similar to a key opening a lock (see Figure 17). They modified messages of pain or pleasure going to the brain. These locations on brain cells are

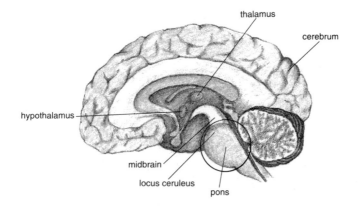

thalamus

cerebrum

hypothalamus

midbrain

locus ceruleus

pons

FIGURE 16: THE MIDBRAIN AND THE PONS
Although it is a small area in the base of the brain, the
midbrain is a regulatory center for all body processes.
It is located below the massive cerebrum, thalamus, and
hypothalamus, and above the pons, which is the bridge from
the spinal cord into the brain. The body and brain are linked
to each other by nerve fibers traveling between the pons and
the midbrain. The locus ceruleus is a small area of blue-colored
tissue located in the pons. It communicates the body's
condition of well-being or illness to the midbrain, which
in turn regulates the body's reaction and distributes the
information to areas of the brain.

known as endorphin receptors. Once a receptor is
filled, the communication of pain diminishes.

When the brain cells in the locus ceruleus were
exposed to heroin, scientists found that this area of
the brain became hyperactive; that is, more receptors
on nerve fibers there reacted with the heroin molecules. The opiate in effect was competing with the
endorphins for receptor sites in the brain. As heroin
use continued, the production of endorphins gradually decreased in the brain of the addict. More receptor sites became active in the locus ceruleus, and

57

1) Normal
Before the use of heroin, endorphin receptors on the membranes of the locus ceruleus are activated by endorphin molecules.

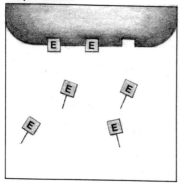

2) Beginning of addiction
After exposure to heroin for a few days, the membranes become more active than usual, and more receptors are activated by heroin and endorphin.

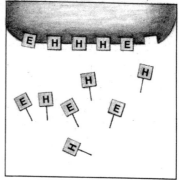

3) Addicted
After several weeks, normal production of endorphin molecules drops off, heroin reacts with the endorphin receptors, and even more receptors have been activated.

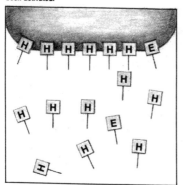

4) Withdrawal
Endorphin production ceases as one of the effects of heroin addiction. During withdrawal from heroin, in the absence of endorphin, a sense of illness is transmitted to the brain, and then to the body.

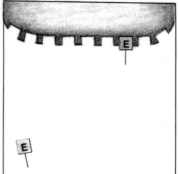

FIGURE 17: OPIATE RECEPTORS IN THE BRAIN

This is a theoretical model that explains what happens to the locus ceruleus in the pons during drug addiction and withdrawal. The membranes of the locus ceruleus have cells that produce endorphin, and cells that have receptors for endorphin. At the most basic level, when an endorphin molecule locks into a receptor, it communicates a sense of well-being in the body. Opiate molecules react with endorphin receptors.[1]

these sites were primarily being filled by the opiate. If the amount of heroin in the blood of the addict began to decrease, the abundance of active receptor sites in the locus ceruleus were not being filled by endorphins. The result was a reaction called withdrawal, a process that occurs after the brain has become accustomed to the presence of a drug. Withdrawal has very harsh psychological and physical consequences.

From the First Minute to the First Hour

It takes about a minute for the first dose of heroin injected into a vein to reach the brain. However, the first reaction that a person has to heroin is not the sleeplike, dreamy state of the addict. The initial sensation is nausea. Most people vomit when they try heroin for the first time. This is the body's reaction to the presence of poison. After the vomiting has stopped, the user will sense a warm surging. This is followed by a feeling of euphoria that is different from that experienced by the cocaine or crack cocaine user. Instead of a feeling of intense well-being, the euphoric reaction that takes place at the receptors in the locus ceruleus is characterized by feelings of satisfaction, relief, and physical warmth.

As first time users feel the effects of the heroin wearing off, they remember the intensity of the feeling they experienced during a period of about an hour. If they find it appealing, they will pursue it by buying another dose or "fix" of heroin and injecting it. This second experience, and possibly a dozen more, will have the warm intensity they enjoyed so much.

From the First Day to the First Two Weeks

With repeated injections over a period of a few days, users develop a love affair with heroin. They will still experience the intensity of physical and emotional feelings with the drug. They may not notice, after about a week, however, that they now need more of the drug to get the feelings they enjoy so much, and are a little anxious when the drug is no longer in their systems about 8 to 10 hours after the last dose. They will start to yawn a little more often. They may feel a slight craving they did not feel before.

Within the first week several changes begin in the locus ceruleus of users. The severity of these changes varies with the individual and depends upon the size of the dose. However, all users have the same physical reaction. More receptors in the locus ceruleus react with heroin molecules: its hyperactivity increases to two, three, or four times the number of receptors that were originally filled when the drug was first taken. The body's natural defense system against pain—the endorphins—is being replaced by an outside chemical.

We normally take the function of the endorphins for granted. We learn to ignore life's minor lumps because we are used to the idea that they will simply "go away." We also take our feelings of pleasure for granted. Whenever we eat, drink, accomplish, or feel things that are pleasurable, we assume that this is a normal part of life. The use of heroin changes all that. The drug is now being used by the cerebrum and midbrain in the control of pain and the communication of pleasure.

The Onset
of Withdrawal

By the end of the second week, the amount of heroin required to create the feelings the user has learned to love has multiplied three or four times. Now, within 8 to 10 hours of the last injection, users begin to experience feelings of dysphoria that are similar to those experienced by crack cocaine and cocaine addicts, except these feelings are not only emotional but physical as well, and signal the beginning of withdrawal symptoms.

Heroin users now feel a craving, as well as a gnawing anxiety and a deep restlessness that cannot be overcome. They start to sweat. Their noses run. Their eyes become watery and runny. When they sleep, if they can sleep at all without having the drug in their body, that sleep is restless and broken. These are all moderate heroin withdrawal reactions.

If the craving is powerful, withdrawal involves more body processes. Users feel aches and pains in their muscles and joints, experience hot and cold flashes, and become nauseous and vomit. They have diarrhea, abdominal cramps, and a slight fever.

The only thing that stops these feelings is another dose of heroin. But this time the dose they have been taking, or even a larger dose, does not give them the feeling of pleasure they learned to love. The injection only provides some sleepy relief of the craving and all of the physical reactions that accompany withdrawal. The heroin honeymoon is over. The addiction has begun.

Heroin is able to create a feeling of intense pleasure only as long as endorphins are present. The irony of heroin addiction is that it gradually leads to severely diminished endorphin production in the locus ceruleus. As more of the drug is required to give the feelings of warm, intense satisfaction, the ability to produce those feelings is in the process of shutting down.

From the First Two Weeks to the First Year
With the passage of time, the symptoms of heroin withdrawal that occur between doses, or "fixes," in-

crease in severity. The addict's life becomes an on-going pursuit of the drug. The user exposes himself or herself to the lifestyle that surrounds heroin. Not receiving any drug for the money spent, or purchasing inferior quality mixtures of the drug, is a constant possibility. The hunger for heroin is not linked to violent crime as much as it is to robbery, burglary, and prostitution.

Causes of Death

The symptoms of withdrawal can be violent and very painful.

It is very difficult to overcome heroin addiction. Return to the drug after breaking its grip is common. The most difficult phase of rehabilitation usually takes place over a period of 7 to 10 days. During this time the hyperactivity of the locus ceruleus begins to decrease. Endorphin production begins to increase, but very slowly. The period of time it takes to reach the normal level of endorphin production varies from person to person.

Overcoming the lifestyle of addiction is also difficult. More than 70 percent of all addicts who attempt to overcome heroin abuse return to use of the drug. All of the steps associated with buying and taking the drug have completely filled the life of the addict. To return to a more normal life, an addict must constantly resist all of the behaviors and memories of addiction. Breaking away from friends who are addicts is the most difficult part of overcoming addiction.

Deaths caused by heroin overdose are usually the result of other drugs, poisons, or impure compounds used to dilute the drug. On the black market, the possibility of avoiding contaminated heroin does not exist.

Besides the physical reactions of withdrawal, there are problems with blood clots and infection linked to self-injection and needle-sharing.

An addict can develop "tracks," evidence that veins have collapsed under the skin. It is possible that a small amount of blood can clot where the needle has entered a vein. If this clot breaks free and travels through the bloodstream, it can become trapped in one of the smaller vessels of the brain, and form an embolism, or blockage shutting off blood flow. Without blood and the oxygen it carries, an area of the brain will die. If that area of the brain is responsible for control of an arm, a leg, or the ability to see, hear, speak, and add numbers, the person will lose that particular ability. Very often this loss will be permanent. If the vessel in the brain bursts, death may follow in a matter of seconds. A blood clot that forms in the heart can lead to a few minutes of agony as the heart goes into shock and stops.

There are a number of infections carried in the blood that will cause the addict's death, slowly or quickly. The greatest tragedy is if a needle is shared with another addict who is infected with HIV, the virus that causes AIDS. Other infections that can be passed among heroin addicts are the same as those that are passed by IV cocaine addicts. These infections destroy the liver, the lungs, the heart, and the muscles.

4

CANNABIS: MARIJUANA AND HASHISH

Many young people believe marijuana and hashish are not dangerous drugs. Their belief is based on brief personal experience and the experience their friends have had with these drugs. Suggesting that these drugs are addictive usually invites an argument. Marijuana and hashish addicts are always threatened by information about addiction—they avoid it or simply stop listening.

Very few young people who consistently use these drugs will accept the fact that they are addicts, even if they have cravings. They do not associate this effect with the familiar portrait of the crack or heroin addict, the heavy smoker, or they heavy drinker. Today, the health risks associated with *cannabis* use are becoming accepted and are considered as serious as those associated with tobacco and alcohol abuse.

At one time, no one believed that tobacco and alcohol were dangerous, addictive drugs. These drugs were, and still are, socially accepted, permitted by law, and supported by multi-million-dollar industries. It took 60 years before people started listening to scientific evidence about tobacco and alcohol abuse. It is only in the past ten years that people have begun to accept the very real dangers of cancers and respiratory diseases caused by smoking and liver diseases caused by excessive drinking.

Marijuana and hashish are estimated to be a $10 billion industry.[1] This makes it the third leading commodity in the United States, where 62 million people have experimented with marijuana at least once, and there are currently 18.2 million users. Marijuana is very often the first illegal drug that young people take. The age of first time users has dropped from eighteen in 1965 to between eleven and fourteen today.

Out of all illegal drugs, marijuana has the most complex chemical effect on the body. Marijuana does not contain one drug but many, and is the least understood of all abuse drugs because accurate research results have only recently become available. The research on the effects of marijuana conducted in the 1960s was very limited, unrealistically planned, and poorly executed. Rather than comparing the mental and physical performance of nonusers and consistent users, for example, researchers at that time compared nonusers with occasional users. This led to underestimating the *toxic* effects of the drug and how addictive it can be. We now know marijuana affects every organ system in the body.

The drug strength of marijuana has changed considerably over the past twenty-five years. Laboratory analyses have shown that the marijuana available in major cities throughout the world today is five to fifteen times more powerful than that sold in the 1960s. Also, the addictive and psychological effects of the new crops of marijuana are greater than those in the past. It now appears that marijuana plays a key role in confusing or disturbing the judgment of users during the critical seconds preceding an automobile accident or a violent argument.

The average number of times marijuana is smoked each day, as well as the amount used, has risen sharply since the 1960s. Also, marijuana today is rarely used by itself, as it was during that era. Taking marijuana with one or more drugs at the same time, such as alcohol (most often beer) or cocaine, is more common today than ever.

Doctors are seeing more patients showing the serious and long-lasting effects of marijuana taken in combination with other drugs. Among people between the ages of fifteen and twenty-four, there has been an increase in violent deaths as a result of accidents, suicides, and homicides. The number of autopsy reports showing the concentration of marijuana as higher than other drugs in the blood of victims has been steadily increasing. A relationship between the drug and these deaths is taking shape.[2]

Marijuana may also play a key role in a user's life when suicide becomes a way out of depression, a feeling of extreme sadness or worthlessness that may or may not be related to actual events in life. It is a disorder of the emotions that develops when a person is very disappointed and frustrated. If the person cannot find reasons for feeling this deep sadness, the depression simply worsens. Many people who suffer from depression cannot do anything about it because the chemistry of their brains is different from normal brain chemistry. This problem is very common.

Studies of the brain have shown that clinical depression is a biological disease based on chemical disorders. Research has shown that the problem lies in the complex system of neurotransmission, the chemical sending of signals from nerve cell to nerve cell in the brain. Doctors have only recently found ways of treating this emotional disease with compounds that stop the reactions in the brain that cause this deep sadness.[3]

It is believed that marijuana alters the chemicals involved in neurotransmission. Marijuana causes reactions in the brain that create depression. It is one of the effects of the drug any user will experience as it wears off. This can push a person who has this emotional disease into feeling even worse.

HISTORY AND COUNTRIES
OF ORIGIN[4]

The scientific name for the marijuana plant is *Cannabis sativa*. More commonly referred to as cannabis, the plant's properties have been known for almost 5,000 years.

Some scholars believe that the Old Testament contains references to cannabis: the plant called honeywood in Samuel and calamus in the Song of Solomon. The first record of cannabis as an herbal medicine comes from China, in a text written for the emperor Shen Nung in 2737 B.C.

Different parts of this plant have been used for a variety of purposes. Cannabis is a plant that has separate male and female genders. The male plant is tall and narrow with a thick stalk or shaft that can be shredded to make hemp, which has been used in the weaving of rope, carpets, sails, linen and canvas. The stems and seeds of the male and female plants have been used in the manufacture of soap, paints, and birdseed. The female plant has longer branches, is wide, full, and very leafy. Its flowers, leaves, and seeds contain the active chemicals that have intoxicating effects and medicinal properties.

First cultivated in Asia, cannabis's use spread to India about 2000 B.C., where it was used in religious ceremonies. The priests controlled its cultivation and distribution to keep secret their method of brewing

The hemp plant, Cannabis sativa, *commonly known as cannabis. Marijuana is made from its dried leaves and flowers.*

the leaves of the plant into a liquid called *bhang*. From India, knowledge about cannabis spread to the Middle East, where a solid form of bhang, known as hashish, was extracted from marijuana leaves and concentrated to produce hashish oil.

From the Middle East, cannabis spread to Greece and Italy. It is mentioned by Homer in the *Iliad*. The famous Greek physician Galen described using cannabis to treat earaches. Herodotus, the Greek historian, wrote that enemy soldiers from the East, before a battle, threw it upon red hot stones to release its vapors, which they inhaled.

Islam does not permit the manufacture or use of alcoholic drinks. This may have supported acceptance of hashish in Arabia around A.D. 500. From about 900 to 1200, during the Arab invasions of the Mediterranean region, cannabis was introduced in Egypt, Tunisia, Algeria, and Morocco.

Arabia was the area of the world where hashish gained another meaning: it is the root of the word "assassin." A group of men in Arabia, who called themselves The Hashishan ("the men of Hashish"), used the drug for their work because it helped them maintain the frame of mind required for what they did. They were professional assassins. In 1378 the ruler of Arabia determined that hashish had a detrimental effect on his people and outlawed its use. Anyone found growing or using the plant was to have his teeth pulled out as punishment. In 1600 an Egyptian historian wrote about hashish as an addictive drug that had contributed, from 1400 to 1500, to the decline of Egyptian society.

During the colonial period, 1450 to 1850, cannabis was introduced to Italy, France, and Spain, and was introduced to South America by the Spaniards in 1545, when they began growing it in Chile to harvest hemp for making rope. It is possible that more than

50 years earlier, Africans, who were skilled in the use of cannabis for medicinal and intoxicating purposes, brought it with them to Brazil aboard Portuguese slave ships.

Hemp was brought to Jamestown, Virginia, by English settlers in 1611. It was introduced in New England in 1629. In 1736 Carolus Linnaeus assigned it the name *Cannabis sativa.* (Linnaeus was the Swedish botanist responsible for creating the classification system for plants and animals we use today.)

The modern medical use of cannabis began in 1839 with the recommendation of Dr. W. B. O'Shaughnessy, for use as a drug with the ability to control *convulsions,* stop pain, and relax the muscles. He first saw the drug used in Calcutta, India. Sir William Osler, a famous Canadian physician who also practiced in the United States, recommended cannabis for the treatment of migraine headaches.

In 1840 Dr. Jacques Joseph Moreau, a French scientist, experimented with hashish by eating it and rediscovered its ability to cause intoxication. He introduced the drug to several friends who were artists and writers. They formed a group called "The Club of the Hashish Eaters". Dr. Moreau is also known as the father of *psychopharmacology,* the study of the effects of drugs on behavior and personality.

The *U.S. Pharmacopoeia,* which lists selected medicines and their dosage for use in the United States, cited several different marijuana preparations manufactured by such drug companies as Parke-Davis, Squibb, Lilly, and Burroughs Wellcome from 1850 to 1941.[5]

In New York in 1857, Fitz Hugh Ludlow published *The Hasheesh Eater.* This book talked about his experiences with the drug. After a short time, as with opium, hashish houses were established in major cities of the United States.

70

Cannabis use spread throughout the United States during the 1920s. It was very popular during this era, also known as the Roaring Twenties and the Jazz Age. The interest in cannabis was cultivated by two influences. One was Prohibition, when the use and manufacture of alcoholic beverages was banned. The other was returning soldiers and sailors, from Mexico, Cuba, Jamaica, and Panama, who brought the drug back with them. The term *"reefer,"* the name for a marijuana cigarette, was coined by the sailors of this time. The name comes from "reefing a sail," the process of rolling up a sail during a storm so that less sail area will be exposed to a strong wind.

The first commissioner of the Federal Bureau of Narcotics, Harry J. Anslinger, drove through the passage of the Marijuana Tax Act of 1937. This law made marijuana trafficking illegal and a form of tax evasion. Anslinger was also responsible for a film entitled *Reefer Madness.* It portrayed youthful marijuana users as crazy people and insane killers, and was used to influence parents, teachers, and teenagers throughout the nation. Combined, these tactics were effective in ending the popularity of marijuana among U.S. teenagers and young adults.

Widespread use of cannabis throughout the United States recurred in the 1960s. This era, in some ways similar to the 1920s, was a time when all values were being questioned and overturned by a "counter-culture," whose members called themselves hippies and associated the use of marijuana and LSD with the search for inner fulfillment and personal freedom. Marijuana use became so widespread that legalization was suggested by a group of lobbyists in Congress. This step was never taken. Instead, the possession and use of a very small quantity of the drug was decriminalized. In 1970 the Comprehensive Drug Abuse and Prevention Control Act softened the penalties for possession and use of small amounts of cannabis in all of its forms.

At one time, laughter was the popular reaction to the idea that marijuana is addictive. Laboratory studies now suggest that all forms of cannabis, when used regularly, are addictive. Marijuana, hashish, and hashish oil are not individual drugs. They are crude, primitively prepared combinations of drugs made from the cannabis plant.

Cannabis is a weed, and is able to adapt to different environments and different soils. However, the plant is not a stable species. It will produce different amounts of its compounds depending upon the conditions of its environment. Botanists have identified more than one hundred varieties. No two plants of the same variety produce the same chemicals in the same amounts. Samples taken from different parts of the same plant also vary in their chemical content.

HOW CANNABIS IS USED

All forms of cannabis can be smoked or eaten. The leafy product, marijuana, is usually smoked. Hashish can also be smoked and can be mixed into foods. Hashish oil can be spread on a cigarette and smoked, added to marijuana, or mixed into foods.

Depending upon size, shape, and color, the female and male cannibis plants can be separated into three categories of drug strength: (1) the drug type that produces the most *THC* (this is dried and smoked); (2) the weak drug type that produces less THC (this is used to make hashish); (3) the fiber type that produces very little THC (this is good for making rope).

Hashish is made by collecting the resin given off by the leaves of the plant. It can also be made by boil-

Marijuana is smoked
in cigarette form
or in a pipe.

ing parts of the crushed plant in water, which is evaporated. The brownish black resin that remains is
pressed into balls, cakes, bricks, and other forms.
Hashish oil, distilled from the leaves of the plant by
boiling them with alcohol, resembles a very dark,
thick syrup.

CANNABIS AND
THE BODY[6]

Cannabis contains 421 chemicals. Among them is a
group of intoxicating chemicals with the shorthand
name THC. The most powerful is delta-9-THC. These
are *psychoactive* chemicals, or *hallucinogens,* drugs
that exert their effect on the mind, behavior, and
personality.

About 1 percent to 6 percent of a typical marijuana plant is made of psychoactive THC chemicals.
Hashish, or hash, contains 10 percent to 15 percent
THC; hashish oil, 15 percent to 30 percent. However,
since the late 1970s, new strains of cannibis have
been developed that are 6 percent to 14 percent
THC. In the 1960s, a "joint," or "reefer" contained
about 10 mg of THC. Today, a joint of high-quality
(high-strength) cannabis can easily contain 100 mg to
150 mg of THC, 10 to 15 times the potency. A joint of
average-strength marijuana contains approximately 60
mg of THC. Heavy users usually smoke three to ten
joints per day, depending upon the quality of the marijuana and the length of time the user remains high
after smoking. Heavy users take in from 180 mg to
600 mg of THC each day.

Years ago, marijuana was thought to be unsafe for
recreational use. Now, it is a known fact. Laboratory
tests have shown that a user who takes 179 mg of
THC per day for 11 to 21 days will go into withdrawal
if the smoking is abruptly stopped. The withdrawal
experienced is similar to that for cocaine and heroin.[7]

From the First Eight
Seconds to the First Day

When marijuana, hashish, or hashish oil is smoked, each requires eight seconds to reach the brain, as is the case with crack or opium. The first reaction of the brain to the drug is a sense of euphoria. However, with continued use this immediate euphoria shifts to paranoia and depression. Addicts experience a state of confused emotions that can interrupt their thinking. To relieve this effect, they will use less cannabis or cannabis of lesser strength in combination with cocaine and alcohol.

The drug reaches its peak effect on the user's brain within 10 minutes and decreases slowly over a period of two to three hours. Cannabis cooked into food and eaten takes effect in approximately 30 minutes to 2 hours and decreases over a period of 6 hours.

During the first 30 minutes, users experience many physical reactions to the most powerful psychoactive ingredient, delta-9-THC, and the other chemicals in cannabis. This will depend upon their body weight, the strength of the drug, and the seriousness of their addiction.

Reactions will include all or any combination of the following physical effects:

1. Increase in heart rate (number of beats per minute)
2. Sudden increase in heart rate (tachycardia)
3. Initially increased peripheral circulation (increase in blood flow to areas of the body farthest from the heart: skin, hands, feet)
4. Decreased blood flow sometime later to the hands and feet (cold)
5. Decreased skin temperature (chills)
6. Expansion of the bronchi
7. Reddening of the eyes (expansion of blood vessels in their outer tissues).

8. Decreased pressure inside the eyes (eyes become smaller; eyelids droop)
9. Decreased respiration (decreased oxygen supply to the brain; increased carbon dioxide in the blood)
10. Slowing of brainwaves (decreased communication in the brain)

From the First Week to the First Month

The psychoactive drugs in marijuana are more soluble (or easily dissolved) in fats and oils than in water. For this reason, delta-9-THC easily enters the fat cells of the body.

Fats and oils are normally stored in the body's fat cells for use later as a source of energy. In cannabis users, the psychoactive delta-9-THC will remain in these cells for approximately 60 days. When the fat is used for energy, THC is slowly released back into the bloodstream. Heavy users may experience THC intoxication after strenuous activity even though they have not used the drug recently, and people can test positive for marijuana use even if they have not used the drug over a period of weeks or months.

CANNABIS AND THE BRAIN[8]

During the past ten years, research has revealed how THC may affect brain chemistry. There seem to be specific chemical pathways of THC addiction in the brain. Experiments involving the stimulation of areas of the human brain with electrodes suggest these pathways may be located in the *limbic reward system* of the brain. The sensations of pleasure described by subjects in these experiments are very similar, and at times the same, as those related by cannabis users when describing the effect of the drug.

The limbic reward system is responsible for moods and survival. In other words, this area of the brain produces feelings of pleasure during and after activities that help to keep one healthy, alive, and in a good mood. The emotional states that are produced by the limbic system are called drive states. Examples are the emotions and actions related to thirst, hunger, and sex, which are very powerful and have been responsible for the survival of humanity for hundreds of thousands of years.

When a person uses cannabis in any of its forms, THC appears to stimulate the drive states of the reward system. It is thought that if the drug is used every day, an association develops in the brain between drive states and their stimulation by THC, which may be altering and redirecting these drive states. The emotional drives for hunger or sex may partially become drives for using cannabis. In a sense, the drug takes control of the limbic reward system.

The brain chemicals involved in drive states are very powerful. The three that are most important are dopamine, *serotonin,* and the endorphins. Dopamine controls feelings of pleasure. Serotonin controls the feeling of being satisfied after eating or other experiences that cause pleasure. (For more information on Serotonin, see pages 98 to 99.) The endorphins play an important role in pleasure, pain, and endurance. (For more information on the endorphins, see pages 56 to 62.) The reactions of these chemicals may be altered by THC to drive addiction-related behavior that includes preoccupation with obtaining the drug, using it compulsively, and forgetting the lifestyle and legal dangers involved in the purchase and possession of illegal drugs.

CANNABIS AND PARANOIA

Paranoia is an intense feeling of fear that does not have a basis in reality and may originate in fear or anger within ourselves. Anger is a very powerful emotion. It causes us to see scenes in our minds that are violent. Very often, these violent ideas come from a previous experience or a memory. Feelings such as pure anger normally are not a part of our everyday world, and usually are not expressed in the wild and primitive form that comes from deep within the human mind. When people physically fight about something, they have lost control of their deep, primitive feelings and are allowing anger to drive their actions.

Why are powerful emotions, hidden beneath our needs and conflicts, set free by a mild hallucinogen such as delta-9-THC? This hallucinogen breaks down the user's judgment and responsible behavior: it affects the mind where these primitive feelings are held in check. Hallucinogens make the mind focus on these inner, hidden feelings. THC causes the brain to color any immediate event with feelings of paranoia.

From the First Month
to the First Year
The total effect of the 421 chemicals in cannabis on the performance of every organ system in the body is not yet completely known. Research on specific organ systems in people who have been using cannabis regularly over a period of one month to one year has produced some important information.[9]

PSYCHOMOTOR EFFECTS
The term "psychomotor" combines the root of "psychology" with "motor functions" to describe the functions of the brain and muscles working together during an activity. The motor functions cover every muscular reaction of the body, including the muscles of the arms, legs, torso, eyes and ears. THC has many effects on psychomotor functions and has been shown to interfere with the psychomotor performance necessary for safely operating a vehicle, whether it be a car or a bicycle.

An example of a psychomotor function is visual tracking ability (VTA), or the ability of the eye to follow an object at high speeds. While driving a car or a bicycle, the brain can normally estimate the amount of time that will pass before overtaking another person in a car or on a bike, or passing an object alongside the road. Cannabis decreases VTA. A person who is high can no longer make normal estimates involving speed and distance.

Another example is the amount of time the human eye requires to recover from a flash of bright light. Let's say a person standing in darkness is startled by a bright light that flashes on and off once. The muscles in the eyes will close the pupils to protect the optic nerve. As the optic nerve recovers from the flash, the pupils will slowly open, so that the eye can make out objects in the dark once again. Cannabis increases the recovery time of the optic nerve, and a person who is high on marijuana will be blinded by headlights at night for a longer period of time than a person who is straight.

People have been tested while driving under the influence of marijuana in both simulated and actual conditions. It has been shown that marijuana decreases coordination by increasing the reaction time of the arms and legs. A person who is high loses 40 percent of his or her psychomotor functions. Of all fatal automobile accident victims in 1987, 16 percent were marijuana users. Marijuana is currently involved in 20 percent of all traffic accidents. Smoking marijuana six times during one month increases the user's chances of having an accident by 250 percent. Among young adults killed in automobile accidents, 37 percent had detectable traces of marijuana in their blood.[10]

The psychomotor effects of cannabis intoxication are not limited to automobile accidents. Cannabis-intoxicated train, bus, and truck drivers, as well as operators of power tools, heavy crane and concrete machinery, have been involved in serious accidents that have injured or killed them as well as passengers or fellow workers. One such accident was a train wreck near Baltimore, Maryland, in 1989, that killed 16 people and injured several hundred in a head-on collision with an oncoming freight train. An investigation revealed that the freight train's engineer, who previously admitted to using marijuana, did not see several track signals warning him to avoid one track and take another so that the passenger train could remain on schedule.

GENETIC AND MUTAGENIC EFFECTS

Genes determine hair color, the way the liver functions, eye color, the size of the lungs and heart—they control thousands of characteristics that permit the human body to function normally.

Genes are attached in chainlike structures called *chromosomes*. These structures carry all the information our cells require for the development and maintenance of the human body. Whether cannabis causes specific changes in chromosomes is unknown. However, more abnormal chromosomes have been found among marijuana users than among nonusers. These abnormal chromosomes return to normal when cannabis is no longer used.

A *mutagen* is a compound, chemical, or drug that causes mutations, or irregular formation of genes in the sex cells. Men or women who use cannabis can produce sperm or eggs that have mutated genes on their chromosomes. The babies born to marijuana users have a much higher rate of incorrectly formed arms, legs, and internal organs.

A mutagen can also cause mutations in the cells of a particular organ, such as the lungs or liver, which can take the form of cancers. The tar produced by cigarette smoke has been shown to cause cancer in animals and humans. Marijuana smoke contains twice the amount of tar found in tobacco smoke and greater amounts of the compounds that are known to cause cancer.

IMMUNE SYSTEM EFFECTS

The immune system defends the body against invading bacteria and viruses, and keeps the cells of the body free of infection by consuming invaders as well as the fragments of dead cells. The system plays an important role in wound healing and the growth of new tissue.

Marijuana has been shown to decrease the production of lymphocytes, the cells responsible for coordinating the immune system. *Macrophages* are cells that clear away dead tissues. The macrophages in the lungs have been shown to become less active in marijuana users. Natural killer cells, which hunt down and destroy invading organisms within the body, are less active in marijuana users. These effects on the immune system stop and the system goes back to normal when all marijuana use stops permanently.

HORMONAL EFFECTS

Hormones are complex molecules that control the development and maintenance of the body. For example, growth hormone is responsible for maturation of the body, which involves the addition of new cells in all of the muscles and organs so that they increase in size, the hardening of the growing ends of the bones, and the development of body hair. It has been shown that people who consistently smoke marijuana do not produce normal amounts of hormones.

After four or more weeks of consistent marijuana use, there is an observable decrease in the hormones responsible for the production of eggs in women and sperm in men. It has been shown that when the menstrual cycle takes place in women who are cannabis users, there are no eggs to remove. The sperm produced by male cannabis users do not swim as powerfully as normal sperm, and die before they reach an egg in the uterus. For these reasons, if a husband and wife are unable to have children and decide to see a doctor about it, the doctor will probably ask them if they have been using cannabis. These hormonal effects may stop when all marijuana use stops permanently. However, delta-9-THC that is trapped in fat cells, and gradually released as the fat is used by the body, can delay the normal production of eggs and sperm for months.

RESPIRATORY SYSTEM EFFECTS

Gases other than oxygen can pass through the walls of the alveoli and blood vessels in the lungs and travel to the brain as well as through the body. For example, if people spend time in a garage that is not well ventilated, where cars are running, they will be breathing in exhaust that is high in carbon monoxide and carbon dioxide. Carbon monoxide will be picked up by a proportion of the red blood cells that are also picking up oxygen at the alveoli of the lungs. When the carbon monoxide reaches the brain, it will interrupt the chemistry of communication between nerve cells and make people feel dizzy and sleepy. Smoking tobacco has a similar effect. Although the dizziness caused by tobacco smoke is offset by the stimulant effect of nicotine, smoking tobacco increases the amounts of carbon dioxide and carbon monoxide in the blood traveling to the brain. However, the amounts of these gases in the blood are 500 percent greater after smoking marijuana.

Marijuana smokers inhale three times as much smoke as cigarette smokers. The interior of their lungs is coated with one-third more tar than cigarette smokers. More of the ciliated cells lining the bronchi and bronchioles are killed by marijuana smoke as compared to cigarette smoke. Many consistent marijuana smokers develop bronchitis. Doctors usually advise marijuana users to stop smoking immediately because their bronchitis infections, which can continue for months or even years, may lead to serious respiratory infections or disorders, such as walking pneumonia, emphysema, and lung cancer. The effects of marijuana smoke on the lungs are *not* reversible. The lungs never completely return to normal performance.

CARDIOVASCULAR EFFECTS

Some of the compounds in marijuana affect the *cardiovascular system* by causing arteries to dilate, or become wider (see Figure 18), which decreases blood pressure. Other compounds cause constriction or tightening of the muscular walls of the arteries. This combination of effects can cause tachycardia. The muscles of a rapidly beating heart require more oxygen but cannot receive it because the lungs absorb less oxygen when a person is high. These effects are

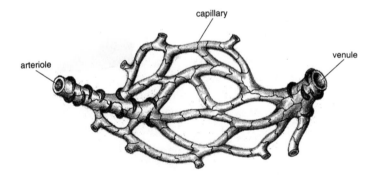

capillary

arteriole

venule

FIGURE 18: ARTERIES, CAPILLARIES, AND VEINS
The dilation (relaxation) or constriction (tightening) of the muscular walls of arteries and arterioles (smaller arteries) will lower or increase blood pressure. The capillaries link the arteries and arterioles to venules (small veins) and veins that do not have muscular walls.

not always dangerous for people with a normal cardiovascular system. However, doctors advise people with heart disease to stay away from marijuana because it can overwork the heart and interfere with many medications that control heart disease, which can be life threatening.

In the United States, 36 million adults have *hypertension,* or high blood pressure. Less than half know they have this condition. Only a quarter of this population seeks medical attention and receives medication. Only an eighth may take medication on time, if they take it at all.[11] The result of marijuana use by people with high blood pressure can be disastrous, especially among those who do not take their medication, or who need to be on medication but do not know it.

DIGESTIVE SYSTEM EFFECTS

In the digestive system, food entering the stomach is treated with acid and enzymes, and softened before it moves on to the intestines. The intestines do most of the work of absorbing nutrients. The colon removes any excess water, returns it to the body, and passes along waste products. The muscular walls of the digestive system move food from one stage to the next by a process called *peristalsis.*

Marijuana, hashish, and hash oil have been shown to cause reverse peristalsis (vomiting) and diarrhea. All cannabis products have been shown to increase the amount of time it takes the stomach to send food to the intestines by decreasing the muscular action of peristalsis. The effect of cannabis on these systems can be powerful enough to change the amount of time it takes for medicines to be absorbed by the body.

All of these effects stop when the use of all cannabis products stops and the fat cells are given time to shed all of their stored THC.

NERVOUS SYSTEM EFFECTS

To date, no structural changes in the brain, the spinal cord, or the nerves leading to the organs of the body are known to be caused by cannabis, although specific performance changes in the nervous system are caused by its psychoactive characteristics. One of these is changes in mood from positive and happy to sad and depressed in only a few minutes or seconds. Another is the loss of a sense of identity or feeling as if we're strangers to ourselves, alone and confused. A third is psychomotor changes—a slowing of reaction time in situations that require well-coordinated movement, such as riding a bicycle or driving a car.

The hallucinogenic effects of delta-9-THC in cannabis cause changes in our ability to judge the passage of time. A minute can seem as long as an hour, and an hour can pass as quickly as a minute.

One of the more dangerous effects of cannabis use is found in the loss of short-term memory, a tendency to forget ideas or things said only moments after they were thought or heard. Long-term use of cannabis can affect recall, or the ability to remember facts about a subject that is under discussion. This can affect performance in school and on the job.

5

PSYCHEDELIC HALLUCINOGENS: PSILOCYBIN, LSD, MESCALINE, AND THE "DESIGNER DRUGS"

Psychedelic hallucinogens are potent drugs that make one see, hear, and feel complete experiences that are happening only in the mind. The term *"psychedelic"* means mind-revealing.

This group of drugs was once thought to resemble the state of being mentally ill. The substances were used to study and treat mental illness until it was determined that they caused a type of change in the brain that is completely different. Psychedelic hallucinogens temporarily alter the chemistry of the brain and the process of perception: the way the mind sees, understands, thinks, and feels. There is no confusion, no loss of memory, no loss of understanding. However, the aftermath of the experience can include flashbacks and personality changes.

HISTORY AND COUNTRIES OF ORIGIN[1]

Psychedelic drugs, such as LSD, are considered by many to be modern drugs. The only thing that is modern about them, however, is the way they are isolated and purified from plant sources by modern methods. There are three groups of drugs that are psychedelic hallucinogens. The first includes LSD or D-lysergic acid diethylamide. LSD comes from a fungus called *ergot,* a microscopic plant that produces the natural LSD-type hallucinogen. Ergot grows on grains such as rye, wheat, and dried corn. Several hundred varieties of ergot contain psychedelic compounds. Another drug in this category is *psilocybin,* which comes from the psilocybe mushroom, or "magic mushroom." The LSD sold on the street can be a synthetic or isolated product.

The second group includes *mescaline,* which is produced from the buttons, or buds, of the *peyote* cactus that grows in the southwestern United States and Central America. The milk squeezed out of these buds is also called peyote.

The third group are the "designer drugs," which are modified amphetamines (see Chapter 6). Amphetamines, also referred to as speed, are stimulants. When other chemicals are attached to amphetamine molecules, the drugs produced are powerful psychedelic hallucinogens. This group includes DOM (STP), MDA, DOET, MMDA, TMA, MDMA (Ecstasy, Adam) and MDEA (Eve).

The history of LSD and other psychedelic drugs spans 3,500 to 5,000 years.

Evidence of the use of psychedelic mushrooms and grains infected with ergot can be found in many religions of the ancient world. The popular belief is that these sources of psychedelic hallucinogens were first used in the religious ceremonies of the Inca and Aztec Indians in South and Central America. Anthropologists have discovered evidence, however, that the first place people ate mushrooms and grains infected with ergot was Siberia, in northern Russia. It is speculated that inhabitants in this area, after seeing animals behaving strangely from eating certain mushrooms or grains, also ate the substances, unaware that they contained psychedelic compounds. While under the effects of the psychedelics, the people believed they were having a religious experience. They associated this powerful, revealing, and sometimes frightening experience with one source: the place, or being, or force that made thunder and lightning, floods and earthquakes, birth and death. Archaeologic evidence shows that after eating psychedelic mushrooms, ancient peoples discovered the ingredient in their urine that caused these experiences and saved the urine to drink at religious ceremonies.

The Rig Veda, a sacred collection of verses of the Hindu religion written some 3,500 years ago, describes experiences caused by drinking a substance called *soma* that is clearly psychedelic in nature. Bible scholars have suggested that the Tree of Knowledge in the Garden of Eden was not an apple tree, but a plant with a similar silhouette—a mushroom. The annual festival at Eleusis, an ancient city outside Athens, Greece, was celebrated with a drink called *kykeon* made of water, mint leaves, and flour. Detailed descriptions of the experiences people had after drinking this mixture suggests the grain that was ground into flour for this drink was probably infected with ergot.

Many psychedelic plants were known in South and North America from pre-Columbian times (before Columbus, 1492). The predecessors of the Aztec Indians, the Toltecs, for centuries used mushrooms containing psychedelic compounds. Morning-glory seeds infected with ergot were used by the Aztec priests and administered to sacrificial victims.

Montezuma established himself as the king of Mexico when he conquered the Aztecs. At his coronation in 1502, the Spanish conqueror's men were not prepared for a drink made by the Aztec priests that contained psychedelic mushrooms and that was used to celebrate important events. Terrified by its effects, the Spaniards attempted to destroy the Aztec religion and drove the use of psychedelic mushrooms underground.

Peyote, the source of mescaline, was known to Indians of Canada, North America, and Central America for many centuries. Texas and Mexico are the areas where it was most widely used, and it is still used in religious ceremonies by Indians in the Sierra Madre of Mexico. Peyote is the center of an Indian religion that developed in the nineteenth century when the Indian way of life was destroyed and their people were forced to live on reservations.

The study of psychedelic hallucinogens in Europe and the United States was confined to the laboratory until the middle of the twentieth century. LSD was first isolated in 1938 by Albert Hoffman, a research scientist. Hoffman accidentally absorbed some of the psychedelic drug through his fingertips in 1943. He wrote in his laboratory notes that he experienced a powerful dizziness and restlessness, as well as vivid hallucinations. His journey, or "trip," into his mind lasted about two hours. Hoffman later experimented with the drug on himself. He swallowed a dose of 250 micrograms, thinking that so small a dose would have a very limited effect. (A microgram is one millionth of a gram.) In his notes he wrote that after 30 minutes he felt fine. At 40 minutes the hallucinogen took effect. This time the experience was far more powerful and lasted for about 12 hours. No other drug had ever been discovered that could be so powerful in such small doses.[2]

In the 1950s, the writer Aldous Huxley experimented with mescaline and described its effects in *The Doors of Perception.* He spoke widely about the subject to psychiatrists, psychologists, and physicians in 1958. At the time of his experimentation, Huxley, who was already blind in one eye, was slowly going blind in the other and was dying of cancer.

Interest in the psychedelics was growing rapidly. There were six papers about the hallucinogens published in scientific journals in 1950. There were 118 papers published in 1956, 220 papers in 1957, and 320 papers in 1958. The number continued to grow until 1965, when LSD was classified as an abuse drug and was no longer available.

Timothy Leary, a psychologist on the faculty at Harvard University, experimented extensively with LSD. He coined the expression "Turn on, tune in, drop out," and became the leader of the psychedelic movement of the 1960s. Leary spoke extensively about LSD and encouraged the counterculture of the time to use the drug. His purpose was to share the self-discovery and the sense of mystical revelation he had experienced. Instead, LSD was used recreationally, along with marijuana and other illegal drugs.

MDMA (Ecstasy) was used for the treatment of couples with emotional and sexual problems. The drug causes the user to feel empathy, or the ability to identify with another person's emotions and ideas. The use of Ecstasy stopped when it was determined the drug did not help people the way it was hoped. It was classified along with all of the "designer drugs" as an illegal substance made with amphetamines. Most of the "designer drugs" are actually mixtures of the amphetamines, PCP, and strychnine. Although MDMA, MMDA, MDA, DOET, and other "designer drugs" may exist, they are difficult to produce due to the expense of the reactants involved.

HOW PSYCHEDELIC
HALLUCINOGENS ARE USED

Psychedelics are usually swallowed. They may be in raw form (as mushrooms or a peyote button), or they may be prepared as tablets or a colored solution placed on small paper squares (blotter acid). Snorting or injecting these drugs is rare, although the Indians of the Amazon use a blowpipe to drive psychedelic snuffs up into the nose and sinuses.

PSYCHEDELIC HALLUCINOGENS
AND THE BODY[3]

Psychedelics have their strongest effect on the brain. The effect on other organs is minimal, except for certain types of rye seed ergot that are powerful hallucinogens and cause dry gangrene in the arms and legs. This is an obstruction of an artery, which stops the flow of blood, as well as the circulatory system's dissolved nutrients, oxygen and the removal of waste, causing the death of tissues. The ergot also causes severe convulsions, or wild movements of the arms and legs, as well as loss of bladder and bowel control. If the area of the brain that controls breathing is affected, users die of suffocation.

From the First Hour
to the First Day

The physical effects of a psychedelic become noticeable approximately 30 to 45 minutes after the drug has been taken. There are four very common reactions:

1. Dilation of the pupils: The black centers of the eyes become as large as when the eyes adapt to a darkened room. With LSD use, the effect lasts

about 8 to 12 hours; this effect varies with other psychedelic drugs.

2. *Hyperreflexia:* An above-normal increase in the speed of reflexes. A *reflex* consists of a message traveling from a part of the body to the spinal cord, from the spinal cord to the brain, from the brain to the spinal cord, and back to the part of the body where the message started (see Figure 19). Touching a hot stove and pulling your hand back before the fingers burn is a reflex action to touching a hot surface. Reflexes happen in a split second; with LSD, they may be even faster.

3. *Piloerection:* The hair on the surface of the skin stands on end; a physical reflex related to fear or anxiety.

4. Tension: A tightening of the muscles usually localized in the neck and shoulders but can involve the entire body; sometimes accompanied by a *tremor,* an involuntary trembling or quivering that can be seen in the hands but may involve many of the muscles throughout the body.

There are eleven other physical reactions to psychedelics. These vary in combination and intensity depending on the particular drug.

1. Loss of coordination: A mild inability to maintain balance; difficulty in performing tasks requiring manual dexterity.

2. Nausea

3. *Ataxia:* Loss of coordination resulting from interruption of nervous system pathways that control a movement. For example, the action of opening a cabinet and reaching for a cup involves nervous system pathways that lead to over fifty different muscles in the hands, arms, shoulders, back,

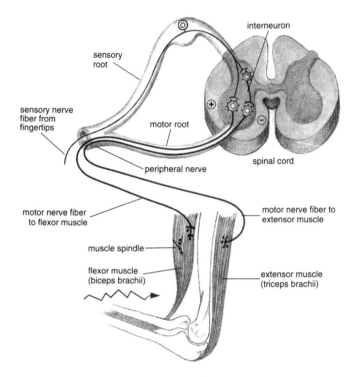

FIGURE 19: REFLEX—STIMULUS AND RESPONSE
When you touch a very hot surface, a message of extreme heat, which is called the stimulus, is communicated by nerves in your fingertips. Within a fraction of a second (at about 150 miles per hour), this message travels to the spinal cord, which relays another message, called a response, all the way back to the elbow that directs the muscles to PULL THE HAND AWAY—*NOW*!

chest, waist, legs, and feet. With ataxia, as the hand reaches for the cup, some muscles will move as they should and others will start movements that are not related, causing parts of the body to move incorrectly.

4. *Paresthesia:* A strange combination of feelings on the skin caused by a drug. For example, it might consist of sunburn, insects crawling, and goose-flesh on the skin all at the same time.
5. Dizziness
6. Weakness: Effort is required to lift the arms or legs.
7. Drowsiness
8. Increased appetite: Some psychedelic hallucinogens stimulate the area of the brain that controls the hunger drive state.
9. Tachycardia
10. Hypertension
11. Increased respiration

These last three effects are related: Tachycardia is a rapidly beating heart; hypertension is increased blood pressure. Psychedelic drugs cause the heart to beat faster and cause blood vessels to contract. The contraction of the blood vessels makes the heart beat even faster as it forces blood through narrower passages. When the heart works harder, the rate of respiration (the transfer of oxygen and carbon dioxide across cell membranes) increases.

**From the First Day
to the First Week**
Tolerance to a psychedelic hallucinogen is established after 3 to 5 days, when higher doses are then required to achieve the same effect. The mind becomes less responsive to the drug; that is, it seems as though the substance no longer has the powerful effect experienced during the first day or two. However, the psychological effects of continuous use during the period of a week can be "mind-expanding" or "mind-blowing" in their results.

THE PSYCHEDELIC HALLUCINOGENS
AND THE BRAIN

These drugs are *sympathomimetic.* The second part of this word, "-mimetic," means to mimic or copy. The first part, "sympatho-," means having to do with the sympathetic division of the autonomic, or involuntary, nervous system. It is called sympathetic because it works together with the brain and the spinal cord to help maintain control of the internal organs and body movements (see Figure 20).

The *sympathetic nervous system* consists of large and small nerve bundles and fibers outside the brain and spinal cord. This division is sometimes called the "flight or fight" division because its activities apply to emergency or stress situations. It reacts by accelerating the heart rate, increasing blood pressure, and diverting blood flow from the skin and internal organs to the muscles of the arms, shoulders, chest, back, and legs that are used in pushing, pulling, carrying, climbing, and running.

A sympathomimetic drug is able to cause chemical communication in the nervous system that mimics or copies the normal communication that occurs between the central nervous system (the brain and spinal cord) and the sympathetic division. The psychedelic hallucinogens can cause a "flight or fight" condition in the heart and skeletal muscles when there is no reason to get ready to fight or run away from danger. The last three physical reactions to the psychedelics listed earlier in this chapter—tachycardia, hypertension, and increased respiration—are part of this "flight or fight" reaction.

HOW MESSAGES ARE SENT
THROUGH THE NERVOUS SYSTEM

Messages to and from the nervous system are made of electrical charges, called impulses, that travel

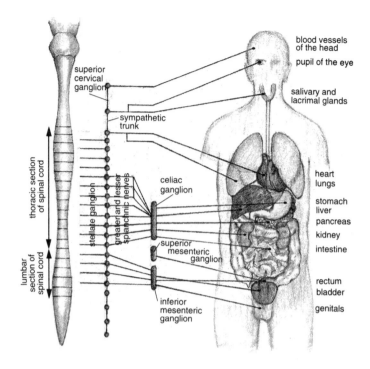

FIGURE 20: AUTONOMIC NERVOUS SYSTEM: SYMPATHETIC DIVISION

This division controls the flight or fight reaction to danger. It is made up of nerves that travel from the spine to the body, and its messages order the following reactions:

1) Release epinephrine from the adrenal glands.
2) Increase heart rate to pump blood to muscles.
3) Decrease activity of internal organs and rush blood to skeletal muscles of the arms, trunk, legs.
4) Focus on information from the senses of sight, hearing, smell, temperature, and touch.

at very high speeds. Normally, an impulse will be barreling down a nerve at about 150 miles per hour, and some nerves can be as much as 3 feet (about 1 meter) in length. Although nerves throughout the body are the pathways for impulses, they do not touch. There is a gap between nerve cell endings called a synapse (see Figure 21). To get across the synapse, an impulse must be carried or transmitted from the end of one nerve to the beginning of the next. This is accomplished by messenger chemicals—*neurotransmitters*—that are located in the synapse between the nerve endings. After a neurotransmitter passes the im-

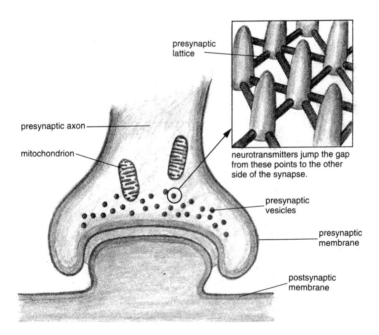

FIGURE 21: THE SYNAPSE
This is the gap between the end of a nerve that is carrying an impulse, or message, and the next nerve. This gap is not empty. It is filled with fluid. The electric charge that is traveling toward the synapse activates a neurotransmitter molecule on one side of the gap. This molecule picks up the electric charge, jumps the gap, transmits it to the next nerve, and the impulse continues along its path.

pulse to the next nerve cell, a message can once again race along to wherever it needs to go.

PSYCHEDELIC DRUGS AND
NERVOUS SYSTEM MESSAGES

Normally, the sympathetic nervous system only becomes involved when the presence of danger is communicated to the brain by emotions and the senses, the nerves in the eyes, ears, nose, mouth, and skin. When no danger is present, neurotransmitters such as serotonin are released to maintain a relaxed mental and physical state, inhibiting sites in the brain that communicate with the sympathetic nervous system. When danger is present, there is serotonin uptake by receptors in the brain, and other neurotransmitters immediately establish contact with the sympathetic division.

The psychedelic drugs are able to fool the brain by taking the place of serotonin at its receptors.[4] When serotonin is replaced by LSD in the brain, the brain reacts as though it received a danger signal and communicates with the sympathetic division of the nervous system, demanding a "flight or fight" reaction: the heart speeds up, digestion slows down, all blood is diverted to the skeletal muscles. The body is prepared to run as fast as it can, or fight as hard as it can. Since this is a false danger signal, the person using LSD will feel excitement, anxiety, and fear without any basis in reality, all caused by the hallucinogen.

The serotonin receptors in the brain where LSD makes contact are responsible for interpreting visual (sight), olfactory (smell), auditory (hearing), and tactile (touch) sensory information. When serotonin is replaced by LSD, the understandable sensory information normally transmitted by serotonin is converted into hallucinations.[5] For example, the gallop, snorting, and odor of a horse are forms of sensory information that serotonin receptors in the brain help us to see, hear, and smell. When serotonin is replaced by LSD, the horse's real movements, the sounds it makes, and its odor are changed into hallucinations—shapes, noises, and odors that have nothing to do with the real world.

PSYCHOLOGICAL REACTIONS

Psychedelic drugs cause the user to experience a false "flight or fight" response. Although physical, it also has emotional characteristics. While there might not be any actual danger present, psychedelic drugs cause the user to remember or re-create emotional situations from the past that were dangerous, and these will completely occupy the person's attention.

Individuals use such words as "euphoria," "panic," and "falling apart" to describe their feelings and how they see themselves. Under the influence of the drugs, their moods can shift with incredible speed from happy to annoyed to sad. Many say that they feel as if they are standing outside their bodies. They can watch what is happening to themselves as though they were another person. They become unsure of their behavior and reactions. They feel that their mind is combining with the universe, and the sense of who they are is exploding into thousands of fragments as though it could be lost forever.

Time is very distorted by psychedelic drugs. Everything seems to move in slow motion because the user's physical reflexes increase in speed along with changes in his or her emotions and moods.

The amount of time the brain can concentrate on anything is cut to a few seconds. Logic, the rational relationship of facts, events, or ideas becomes distorted. When users try to explain something they have seen to another person, their sentences often begin with one subject and end up on another.

The most common psychological long-term effect is a long-lasting feeling of panic. It is impossible for people to control the effects of a psychedelic drug. Users feel as though they are out of control. They have a deep fear of "going crazy" forever. Their judgment is thrown off, as is their ability to tell the difference between a thought and reality. When this is combined with panic, users wish the effects of the drug would end immediately. The sense of panic can be so powerful that some users have jumped out of windows or stepped in front of speeding cars. However, this type of violent reaction to psychedelic drugs is very rare.

Many people have spoken about the positive effects of the psychedelics. Timothy Leary, among others, has said that LSD and other hallucinogens make people see the truth about themselves, their God, and the universe. This deep feeling of religious unity with God is the reason why psychedelic mushrooms and grain infected with ergot were used by many ancient peoples.

However, the psychedelics are mind-revealing drugs. Any hidden problem in a person's past will become the "theme" of the psychedelic trip. If this problem were characterized by fear, guilt, or shame, that will be the overall feeling of the experience. Instead of remembering this feeling for a few seconds as a painful moment that is a normal part of life, the feeling will be turned up to full intensity for 8 to 12 hours. The result is not positive. If a young man has emotional problems related to painful memories, and his ability to remain in control of his emotions is stripped away, any disease that is lurking within him can rise to the surface of his personality. The psychedelic experience can push him over the edge into mental illness, usually a form of *schizophrenia*.

FLASHBACKS

When people have visions, hear sounds or voices, sense odd combinations of feelings on their skin, or experience the same emotions they had when they were high on a psychedelic drug, it is called a *flashback*. Flashbacks are common in 25 percent of the people who have used psychedelic hallucinogens. At one time it was thought that flashbacks occurred only in those who had taken many psychedelic trips. It is now known that the occurrence of flashbacks does not depend upon how often the hallucinogen has been used. Instead, it depends upon the intensity of the original drug experience and the emotional condition of the person before he took the drug.

Flashbacks can occur at any time. They can happen when a former user enters a darkened room or is tired, anxious, or high on other drugs. The experience of frequent flashbacks can be both frightening and annoying. It can interrupt a person's concentration with unrelated feelings and impressions.

Currently there is no way to stop flashbacks from recurring. Many attempts have been made with a number of drugs and different forms of psychotherapy, but none has solved this problem.

6   AMPHETAMINES

Amphetamines are stimulants, a group of synthetic (man-made) drugs that act on the central nervous system, increase the activity of the brain, and cause the release of *epinephrine,* a hormone that plays a vital role in survival.[1]

In regularly increasing doses, amphetamines can cause violent behavior and *psychosis,* which is a total break with reality. Amphetamine psychosis takes the form of irrational fear and hallucinations. People who become *psychotic* do not have the ability to meet the normal demands of life, such as studying. They are no longer motivated by participation in work or play. Their behavior is extremely disturbed and motivated by thoughts and feelings that are unrelated to the people and situations around them.

The aftermath of using amphetamines for several days—a "speed trip"—is exhaustion, depression, sleeplessness, and high tension. A person does not have to become an addict to have this experience. Unpleasant physical effects include convulsions, coma, brain damage, and birth defects. In some cases, death is the end result of amphetamine abuse.

Amphetamines are relatively cheap and are thought by some people to be somewhat safe in low doses. Once regular use of an amphetamine is begun, however, the individual will develop a tolerance for the drug and require higher and higher doses to achieve its effects. This eventually leads to addiction, with severe psychological and physical consequences.

HISTORY AND COUNTRIES OF ORIGIN[2]

Amphetamines were first synthesized in Germany in 1887. Up until the 1930s the dangers inherent in amphetamines were not known. The drug was sold over the counter by itself and as an ingredient in remedies and elixirs. With a readily available source of the drug, millions of people around the world, including homemakers, students, athletes, and military troops, saw amphetamines as a magic potion that could provide energy or euphoria without harmful side effects.

In 1933 it was revealed that it was not the drugs that were a source of energy: the amphetamines exert part of their effect on the adrenal glands, which normally control the demand for extra energy from the body's own storehouse and increase the heart rate as well as blood flow to the skeletal muscles. Located above the kidneys, the *adrenal glands* produce *epinephrine* (also known as adrenaline), the powerful hormone that plays an important role in the "flight or fight" reaction to danger (see pages 95, 98 and 99). Epinephrine supplies the stimulation required to stand your ground and fight or run for your life.

Amphetamine sulfate was first introduced under the trade name Benzedrine by Smith Kline & French, a pharmaceutical company. It was sold in Europe in the form of inhalers or tablets in 1932 to treat lung congestion. These inhalers brought relief to sufferers of colds, hay fever, and asthma. The first signs of the abuse of amphetamines surfaced when Benzedrine strips were removed from inhalers and soaked in coffee or alcoholic beverages.

It was during World War II that amphetamine use became widespread in Europe. From 1939 to 1946, manufacturers suggested thirty-nine different uses for amphetamines, including night blindness, seasickness, migraine headaches, hiccups, and low blood pressure. The idea that the drug was effective and nonaddictive made it very attractive.

European soldiers were liberally issued amphetamine tablets to fight battle fatigue and boost morale. The British forces were given about 72 million tablets. German panzer troops took amphetamines to maintain physical endurance. Hitler's medical records show that he was being injected with methamphetamine up to five times a day throughout the war. This may have accounted for some of his paranoid ravings.

Japanese troops also used significant amounts of amphetamines. It has been suggested that kamikaze pilots took massive doses of amphetamines before their suicide missions. A survey of Japanese military prisoners after the war showed at least 25 percent were misusing Benzedrine inhalers. The postwar era saw an epidemic of amphetamine use in Japan.

Soldiers returning home to the United States from the war in Europe and the Pacific told of the invigorating properties of amphetamines. A few months after the end of the war, students, athletes, truck drivers, and homemakers were using the drug as "pep pills" rather than for medicinal purposes.

Though the drug was still primarily prescribed by doctors in the United States as an antidepressant and a stimulant for treating *narcolepsy* (pathological sleepiness), obesity, and depression, many people took it to give them more energy. The name "uppers" referred to the lift people would feel after taking amphetamines. Young adults found the drug decreased the need for sleep. It was not until the 1950s that the addictive power of amphetamines was finally revealed.

Amphetamine use was not limited to the general public. The British prime minister Anthony Eden admitted to using amphetamines during the Suez crisis of 1952. During the 1960s, President John F. Kennedy was one among many famous people who turned to the invigorating properties of amphetamines.

In the mid- to late 1950s and early 1960s, American soldiers in Korea and Vietnam mixed amphetamines and heroin to produce "speedballs." This term is now used to describe a mixture of cocaine and heroin. Amphetamines were still being widely prescribed by doctors to help patients fight fatigue and their waistlines. Diet pills were very popular. About 3.5 billion amphetamine tablets, to fulfill a number of uses, were manufactured in 1958 alone. Ironically, in the same year, Dr. Philip Connell published an important study on amphetamine psychosis: the drug was shown to cause paranoia, hallucinations, acute terror, and violent reactions. Still, the prescription of amphetamines for weight loss and fatigue continued for another twenty years before these uses of the drug were discredited.

There was a trend toward intravenous use of amphetamines during the late 1960s. Legally manufactured supplies of injectable methamphetamine found their way into the street markets of New York. The initial availability of injectable amphetamines developed because many doctors believed it was a safer alternative for the treatment of intravenous heroin and cocaine users. The use of intravenous methamphetamine in the Haight-Ashbury district of San Francisco was reported by the media in 1968. The negative effects of a drug that was being used to control heroin addiction began to accumulate: increased blood pressure, psychosis, and suicidal depression. Patients were becoming addicted to amphetamines. After the drug was withdrawn from use in the treatment of addicts, illegal laboratories continued to supply dealers in major cities.

There was a resurgence of amphetamine use among young adults in the late 1970s. During this decade, snorting or sniffing became the popular way of taking amphetamines as well as cocaine and heroin. Amphetamine sulfate quickly rose to the top of the menu of street drugs.

Amphetamines became popular with athletes. The "Sunday syndrome" was identified in studies of football players who used amphetamines to combat the sleepiness caused by narcotic medications for pain, or who took the drug to get hyped up and more aggressive for the next game.

HOW AMPHETAMINES ARE USED

There are three main types of amphetamines: methamphetamine, known as "meth" or "crystal meth"; dextroamphetamine, better known as "dexies" and "go fast"; and levoamphetamine, more commonly called "bennies" and "uppers," usually produced as amphetamine sulfate. Methamphetamine can be snorted or injected. The form that can be smoked is known as "ice." Methamphetamine has twice the potency of dextroamphetamine, which has twice the potency of levoamphetamine.

Most illegal amphetamines used today are in the form of amphetamine sulfate that is part dextroamphetamine and part levoamphetamine. This is an off-white or pink powder with an average purity of 15 percent to 20 percent. The remaining 80 percent to

85 percent of the powder is made up of less powerful stimulants. These can be *caffeine,* which is found in coffee, or drugs like strychnine, a poison that in small doses causes the heart to race and in moderate to large doses causes death. *Inert,* or nonreactive, substances that are commonly added include glucose and vitamin C. Chalk, talcum powder, or other fillers may be present that can cause severe problems in the circulation if the powder is dissolved in solution for intravenous use. These powdered materials can become trapped in the blood vessels of the brain or the heart and cause the death of the user by stroke or heart attack.

An occasional user may consume half a gram over a period of several days, whereas a heavy user with a high tolerance level may take up to eight grams a day.

AMPHETAMINES AND
THE BODY[3]

These stimulants produce feelings of exhilaration, high energy, a sense of well-being, power, and confidence, and an enhanced ability to concentrate on simple tasks. The drugs reduce the need for sleep as well as the need for food since the user's appetite becomes suppressed.

From the First Minute
to the First Hour

When swallowed, the amphetamines take effect within 15 to 30 minutes. A standard oral dose of one 5- to 10-mg tablet of amphetamine may cause physical effects such as rapid, shallow breathing (hyperventilation), increased heart rate (mild tachycardia), and a rise in blood pressure (hypertension). Amphetamine sulphate also causes widening of the pupils, dry mouth, diarrhea, and increased urgency to urinate.

A higher dose of oral amphetamine, up to 20 mg in 24 hours, causes a more intense form of the low-dose effects. Reactions include a consistent feeling of vitality, sweating, headaches, grinding of teeth, jaw clenching, and a fast beating heart (tachycardia). The vessels below the skin contract in response to this drug. The user looks pale, and the hands and feet become cold.

If the drug is injected, its effects are intensified by a sudden sensation in the brain called a rush. An injectable form of amphetamine sulfate is made by dissolving the drug in water. The solution is filtered through cotton wool to remove the chalky ingredients that are used to "cut" the drug. A more powerful rush is obtained by injecting the less easily obtainable methamphetamine. The rush, which has been compared to an electric spasm through the body, lasts barely half a minute.

Amphetamines are especially dangerous for people who have certain preexisting medical conditions. For example, people with heart disease may experience heart attacks. In people with *hyperthyroidism*, an overactive thyroid gland, amphetamines will cause extreme racing of bodily functions that are already accelerated, such as an increased metabolic rate and a rapid heart rate. People with high blood pressure can have a stroke. People who have *glaucoma*, an eye disease that clouds vision and leads to blindness, can become blind more quickly without proper treatment.

From the First Day
to the First Week
Regular users of both oral and injectable amphetamines may go on a "run," a long session of continuous use over several days. They will repeat doses as often as every one to two hours. In this way, users attempt to maintain the exhilaration of the first rush.

By the second day, as tolerance for the drug increases, the effect wears off and the euphoria and boosted confidence can give way to agitation of mind and body. During the run users do not sleep and rarely eat. When the supply of the drug runs out, or exhaustion sets in, broken sleep for 48 hours or more follows. Waking is accompanied by extreme hunger and depression that may be so severe that some users become suicidal. Users can feel lethargic for several days after waking and experience renewed anxiety or panic attacks.

While users find that their concentration has increased, they may focus abnormal attention on single objects, such as road signs while driving at high speeds, or on simple ideas shown by an illustration in a textbook. Complex functions, such as studying for exams or operating automobiles, trucks, and heavy equipment, is not advisable.

Although the amphetamines negatively affect thought, memory, creativity, and judgment, they can actually improve performance on tasks that require little thinking, such as sorting or stacking. The drugs are also effective in helping people to get a sense of reality from everyday tasks after they have lost contact with normal life as a result of neurologic or mental disorders. This was one of their original uses.

Amphetamines have been called effective *aphrodisiacs,* or sexual stimulants. While low doses of amphetamines do appear to enhance sexual feelings and performance, higher doses decrease sensation.

From the First Month
to the First Year
The body can quickly build up a tolerance to amphetamines, particularly if the drug is being injected. The tolerance level determines the dosage that can cause a poisoning reaction, or overdose. The more regularly

the drug is used, the higher the tolerance becomes. With an occasional user this may be 30 to 60 mg, and up to 500 mg with a regular user. Some users have survived several times this amount. The level of tolerance diminishes with abstinence.

Long-term users of amphetamines experience a number of disorders, including chronic sleeping problems, outbursts of temper, an erratic heartbeat, and persistent anxiety. Following continuous use, their bodies need the drug in order to function properly: they regularly crave the physical and psychological high associated with amphetamines. When this condition occurs, users are said to be addicted and, without the drug, will begin to experience withdrawal. Addiction is part of a vicious cycle. Repeated use of amphetamines results in increased tolerance of the drug. A user must then increase the dose to achieve the desired effects. This causes an increase in tolerance until the user becomes addicted. Addiction to amphetamines varies considerably in its intensity from a mildly uncomfortable feeling to an overwhelming need for the drug.

Amphetamines dilate the pupils of the eyes, causing users to have an exaggerated open-eyed look. As more light enters the eyes, amphetamine users become more light-sensitive. They compensate for this by wearing sunglasses throughout the day and in the evening as well to soften the glare of lights. This dilation of the pupils over a long period of time may cause blurred vision. Heavy amphetamine use can damage the small blood vessels in the retina of the eye.

As amphetamines increase the user's level of activity and suppress appetite, the body's supply of fuel (glycogen and fat) is depleted. Users can lose up to 20 percent of their body weight over a period of a few months.

In addition, amphetamines can disturb the development of an embryo. This gives rise to birth defects, malformations, and amphetamine addiction in the newborn. The damaging effects caused by the drugs are irreversible. If the use of amphetamines stops one or two months after conception, it is still too late. Mothers who continue taking amphetamines after the birth are often psychologically unable to provide adequate care. However, a woman using amphetamines may not be able to have a child in the first place. Prolonged amphetamine use leads to severe weight loss. A normal supply of body fat is used as energy for the processes of producing complex molecules such as hormones, repairing body tissues, and building new tissue. Without fuel, a woman's body interrupts processes that are not necessary for survival. She will stop menstruating and become infertile.

AMPHETAMINES AND THE BRAIN

High doses of amphetamines can lead to permanent damage to the brain. Constriction and deterioration of small blood vessels in the brain can lead to a *stroke,* in which part of the brain is damaged or dies as a result of lack of oxygen supply (see Figure 22). The bodily functions controlled by that area of the brain can be lost, leading to paralysis, speech disturbance, memory loss, blindness, and sometimes death.

Amphetamines are similar to the psychedelic hallucinogens in their effect on the brain: large doses or extended use can cause sympathomimetic reactions (see page 95). Users, for instance, will unconsciously scratch themselves to relieve amphetamine paresthesia, a constant itching that users imagine is caused by lice or worms crawling on their bodies. In extreme cases, they may believe that they can feel crystals of amphetamine under the skin. The psychosis can lead to constant, often unconscious rubbing, picking,

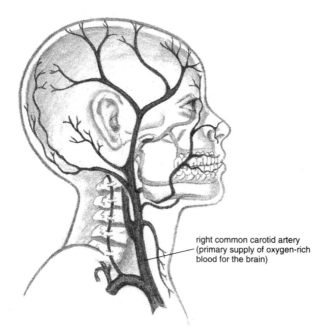

right common carotid artery
(primary supply of oxygen-rich
blood for the brain)

FIGURE 22: ARTERIAL SUPPLY OF THE CRANIUM (SKULL)
The arteries traveling to the brain carry oxygenated blood
that is making its first stop from the lungs. In the neck,
these arteries divide up to feed the brain. If any of these
vessels are injured or blocked, a stroke may result. The
area of the brain that is no longer receiving blood dies,
and any function controlled by this area—sight, hearing,
taste, control of the arms or legs—is lost.

scratching, and digging, resulting in abscesses and
infections.

Users may have visual and auditory hallucinations.
They may believe these are real or may be aware that
they are drug-induced. The hallucinations of paranoid
schizophrenics are usually confined to sounds and
voices. *Amphetamine psychosis* can produce similar
hallucinations. In both cases, the individual may have

conversations with the voices. Schizophrenia and amphetamine psychosis are difficult to distinguish from one another. Clues that the psychosis is amphetamine-induced, however, include the fact that when amphetamine use stops, so do the hallucinations. In amphetamine psychosis, memory remains clear and there is an accurate awareness of time, place, and personal identity. These features are often clouded over in schizophrenia. As with the psychedelic hallucinogens, amphetamine use may trigger an individual's latent schizophrenia.

It was initially thought that only chronic amphetamine users suffered from psychosis. It is now known that low doses, one large dose, or consistent and moderate use of the drug can result in psychosis. Users who have developed amphetamine psychosis will have extreme mood swings. They will be agitated, irritable, and confused, and will have occasional outbursts of uncontrolled and sometimes violent behavior.

CAUSES OF DEATH

Amphetamines that have been "cut," or diluted, may cause a severe allergic reaction called *anaphylactic shock*. This involves the release of *histamine*, a chemical that stimulates the muscles of the stomach and intestines, causes blood vessels to relax and open up, and increases the flow of fluids in the body. Normally, histamine is used in healing processes, such as causing the flow of lymph into a small cut. This provides enough fluid for immune system cells and repair cells to pass through tissues and fight infection. In anaphylactic shock, histamine is produced in such great quantities that too much fluid is released throughout the body, causing tissue swelling and hives. The stress placed on the heart to circulate this greatly increased volume of fluid can cause *heart failure*.

The warning signs of this allergic reaction include

sweating and high temperature. If the amphetamine has been injected, there may also be local swelling. Later, there may be a tightening in the chest and breathing problems as well as a runny nose. The user may even suffocate to death as a result of trachea constriction, which prevents air from reaching the lungs. This is one of the final stages of this shock reaction. The whole process can take anywhere from only a few seconds or minutes to several hours.

If there are any symptoms of anaphylactic shock, the user must get to a hospital where epinephrine, the body's antidote for excessive histamine release, can be injected before convulsions begin. This will work if the reaction can be stopped before the last stages of anaphylactic shock set in. If treatment is begun too late, the individual will most likely die.

Injecting amphetamines with reused syringes and needles exposes the individual to the threat of infection, resulting in abscesses under the skin. Severe cases can lead to infections of the liver (hepatitis) and the envelope of tissue that surrounds the heart (endocarditis). Sharing needles can also contribute to transmission of HIV, the virus that causes AIDS.

The typical signs of an amphetamine overdose include muscle spasms, a racing pulse, and high temperature. These are the results of altering the body's temperature-regulating center in the brain and excess heat that is generated by increased muscle activity. A severe overdose ends in convulsions or coma. When death occurs it is usually as a result of a blockage in the circulatory system by one of the compounds used by dealers to cut or dilute amphetamines. One reaction is *cerebrovascular spasm:* the blood vessels leading to the brain constrict long enough to cause the entire brain to die of a lack of oxygen. Others are stroke and heart failure.

Hyperthermia is an extremely high fever that can

be caused by amphetamine additives. The temperature of the body rises so high that the chemical reactions in the brain stop taking place. Every reaction in the body has a specific temperature range, and when the temperature drops below that range, or rises above it, crucial chemical reactions simply stop.

7 PHENCYCLIDINE (PCP)

Phencyclidine, or PCP, is more commonly known as "angel dust." It has very powerful hallucinogenic effects and is sometimes grouped with the psychedelic hallucinogens (see Chapter 5). It is also a stimulant and is often included among the sympathomimetic drugs (cocaine, amphetamines). PCP is a totally different drug that has many side effects, and these vary in type and intensity depending upon the size of the dose. It is a drug that has been associated with crimes of extraordinary violence.

PCP is one of the most powerful *dissociatives,* mind-altering drugs that cause dissociation. In dissociation, part of a person's personality dominates his or her behavior. To the person under the influence of PCP, the feeling is that a part of himself is functioning independently, or belongs to someone else. The effect of the drug is a deep sense of fear, distrust, and rage. There is behavior that makes the person seem schizophrenic. Frightening thoughts are no longer seen as just thoughts. Instead, for hours or days, they seem as real as the outside world.

After marijuana and other cannabis derivatives,

PCP is the most commonly used illegal drug, ranking above cocaine and the amphetamines. More often than not, the people who use PCP do not know they are taking this drug. Because PCP has effects that are similar to many other illegal drugs, it is used by illegal drug manufacturers, dealers, and pushers as a substitute.

In its white powdered form, PCP has been sold as amphetamine, cocaine, DMT, Ecstasy, morphine, heroin, LSD, mescaline, and THC. Dissolved in a solution, it can be sprayed on oregano leaves that have been bleached to remove their aroma and sold as high-potency marijuana. The same solution can be sprayed on dried mushrooms, available in any supermarket, and sold as psilocybin, or magic mushrooms.

HISTORY AND COUNTRIES
OF ORIGIN[1]

PCP is an anaesthetic that was originally developed in the mid-1950s by Parke-Davis Laboratories, a reputable U.S. pharmaceutical firm. In 1959, before the drug was approved for use in humans, animal studies of PCP showed it had a serene, numbing effect. During the early 1960s, however, there were a number of cases reported that caused the drug to be removed from use in medicine. These were cases of extreme agitation, dysphoria, hallucination, rage, and *delirium* (a severely confused mental state characterized by anxiety, tremors, delusions, and hallucinations).

The idea that PCP could bring a person to the edge of sanity made it interesting to the counterculture of the 1960s. PCP was reissued in 1967 as a tranquilizer strictly for use in animals but became a popular street drug only three months after it was made available to veterinarians. The people who first sold the drug in the Haight-Ashbury district of San Francisco called it the "peace pill." In six months it was being sold illegally in major cities nationwide. PCP acquired a variety of names: "angel dust" on the West Coast, "crystal" on the East Coast, "hog" or PCP in the South and Midwest. However, the popularity of PCP was short-lived. After PCP was associated with some particularly gruesome murders, its use declined in 1968 as quickly as it had risen in 1967.

In 1969 the use of phencyclidine once again rose across the country, but people buying the drug thought they were purchasing cocaine, heroin, amphetamines, THC, LSD, or very potent and expensive marijuana. The use of PCP as a substitute for other drugs continued to rise during the 1970s, when it accounted for 25 percent of all psychedelic drugs sold on the street. During this decade, the crimes committed while under the influence of PCP increased in their severity. People were found dismembered, ground into hamburger, and hacked to death with axes, hatchets, meat cleavers, or machetes.

During the mid-1980s, compulsory drug testing by the U.S. government and major corporations became necessary because of an estimated $25 billion in losses caused by employee absenteeism, bad decisions on the job, accidents in the industrial workplace, and employee theft. The illegal drug laboratories that were making PCP, wanting to protect their market, developed PHP. This is a variation of PCP that cannot be detected by the normal laboratory methods that test for illegal drug use. Within six months it was in use nationwide.

HOW PCP IS USED

Illegal drug producers and dealers found that PCP could be secretly sold in place of higher-priced drugs.

It could be snorted, so it was sold as cocaine. It could be made into a solution and injected in the same way as the opiates, so it was sold as morphine and heroin. Since it could be taken in pill form, it could be sold as anything from the amphetamines to the psychedelics and THC. It could be smoked without losing any of its potency, so it was—and most often still is—sprayed on marijuana and sold as high-grade Colombian marijuana with a powerful kick. PCP could turn a poor-grade crop, sold at $50 to $100 per ounce, into a major money-maker selling for $250 to $350 per ounce.

The high prices charged for potent marijuana, cocaine, and opium make PCP very profitable when it is substituted for these drugs. The cost of making PCP is negligible. All that is needed is a toilet tank full of water restricted from normal use. It becomes the factory. Into the bowl is dumped a catalytic converter obtained from an automobile, or a handful of nickels, and a few very inexpensive chemicals. It is left alone for one week. The liquid is then siphoned or pumped out of the toilet bowl, the water is evaporated, and the powder that remains is PCP. If there is any concern about a police raid, the makers just flush the toilet. This is still the method of choice for the manufacture of PCP.

PCP AND THE BODY[2]

PCP is different from all other drugs in the timing of its effect. When injected intravenously, response can be within three to five seconds—faster than any other drug discussed thus far that is used by injection, and faster than any other illegal drug whether it is smoked, sniffed or injected. When sniffed (snorted), the response time varies from 30 seconds to five minutes. When smoked, the drug takes effect in about eight seconds. When injected into a muscle, response occurs within 1 to 2 minutes. When swallowed, PCP takes effect in 20 minutes.

There is a very specific reason why PCP rages are sudden and come in waves. It has to do with the way the drug is absorbed. Drugs that are acidic are able to pass through the stomach lining and the lungs very easily. Drugs that are chemically basic have a tendency to be absorbed very slowly. PCP is a weak base. For this reason, when it reaches the stomach, it mixes with stomach acid, which stops the drug from being absorbed through the stomach lining. After it passes through the stomach and reaches the small intestine, it is in a nonacidic environment. It returns to its original form, can pass through membranes, and is carried by blood vessels from the intestines to the liver, where it is again released into the bloodstream and travels to the brain.

As amounts of the drug are released by the liver, its effects—PCP rages—can be repeatedly observed. The amount of the drug that reaches the brain decreases with each pass through the liver until all of the PCP has been broken down by the body and eliminated.

When PCP is smoked, some of the drug is trapped in the mouth, the throat, the bronchi, and the lungs, so that only 40 percent of it is absorbed by the bloodstream and travels to both the brain and the liver. It is eventually released from the liver again and travels to the brain.

From the First Three Seconds to the First Hour

PCP has a number of specific, simultaneous effects that are combinations of opposites. It causes reddening of the skin, as though a person were very cold, but the skin is wet with perspiration. It stimulates the sensory nerves of the body that respond to touch and changes in temperature, as well as areas of the spinal cord and the brain that receive this sensory information, but it also acts as an anesthetic, decreasing the user's ability to feel pain. It causes the user to feel emotionally agitated, yet at the same time physically relaxed and sleepy. It affects the eyes by making the pupils relax and become enlarged; at the same time, it causes a condition called *nystagmus,* slight involuntary and repetitive side-to-side eye movements that can occur more than sixty times per minute. The number and severity of the emotional and physical effects of PCP depend upon the size of the dose.

With 0.5 mg of PCP, the user will be agitated and very anxious, will perspire heavily, and will feel flushed. At the same time that the mind is racing, the user might go into a trance, holding his or her body in one position without moving for as long as possible. This is a *cataleptic reaction.* Thoughts will be disorganized; there will be irritability along with euphoria. Some visual hallucinations might be experienced.

If the user takes 5 mg to 10 mg, anxiety will be increased, and he or she will be easily excited. The person might run a slight fever. Reflexes will be hair-trigger fast, but speaking will be difficult because PCP has interrupted nerve messages traveling from the speech center in the brain to the tongue. *Myoclonus,* a spasmodic jerking of muscles will come and go. The user might engage in *stereotopy,* an uncontrollable need to carry out the same movement over and over, such as picking up a cup from a table and placing it on another table in the exact same spot, back and forth. Any aggressive advance by another person might cause the user to become uncontrollably violent and he or she might feel a deep need to injure or kill the other person, who seems very threatening.

These are the sensations that have been experienced by normally nonaggressive people who committed murder while intoxicated with PCP.

A dosage of 10 mg to 20 mg will cause the heart to beat erratically. *Encopresis,* the inability to control bowel movements, might be experienced. There will be a fever. Deep feelings of excitement and vivid, visual hallucinations will occur as well as paresthesia, a tingling sensation on the skin combined with the feeling of crawling insects, both caused by stimulation of the peripheral nervous system. Blood pressure will begin rising rapidly as blood vessels contract in response to release of PCP from the liver or lungs. The user will be locked into *hyporeflexia* for periods of time: reflexes will slow to a crawl; climbing a flight of stairs, for instance, will be difficult due to slow movements.

Another reaction might be *opisthotonos,* a sudden clenching of the muscles in the back that will result in the head and legs being pulled back, causing the trunk of the body to arch foward. The user will not be able to stand or lie flat on the ground or on his or her stomach. As a fish out of water flops on its side, the user will be on his or her side, unable to stop the pain of these muscular spasms. Any paranoid feelings present at the beginning of this PCP experience will be multiplied by fear of one's own body and the pain it is causing. Once the spasms pass, the user will feel fearful and physically injured.

If anyone were to make an aggressive advance, the user might murder that person, drifting into stereotypy in the process. According to the evidence accumulated on murders committed under the influence of PCP, the user would want to dismember the attacker and grind, slice, or chop him up, and would repeatedly use the same movements during the crime.

CAUSES OF DEATH

If the user were to take more than 20 mg of PCP, a usually fatal dose, there would not be any ability to communicate at all once the drug took effect. At first the person would become cataleptic: the body would become rigid as fear dominated the emotions. The physical reactions to the drug would follow a definite pattern. The user would begin to convulse, lose control of the bladder and bowel, vomit, the fingers would twist and grip the air, toes would stretch forward and back. Near the end of the convulsions, he or she would drift into a coma, stop breathing, and die.

From the First Day to the First Year

People who use angel dust usually are aware of the dangers inherent in the drug experience, and they try to keep the doses very small. However, there is no way they can determine the potency of the PCP they are buying. Furthermore, it is important to remember that any other illegal drug could also contain PCP. When drugs are mixed, users can accidentally increase their dose of PCP to dangerous or fatal levels.

The effects of PCP can last anywhere from a few hours to over a week. The drug will vary in potency depending upon how much of it is used and the way it is taken.

As the dosage is increased, PCP will either increase or suppress the release of neurotransmitters, the chemicals responsible for carrying messages from one nerve cell to another. The release of neurotransmitters will increase with a small dose of PCP. A larger dose will suppress those same chemicals. Increasing this dose of PCP will cause a combination of effects: a powerful reduction and release of neurotransmitters in waves. A very large dose will stop the neurotransmitters that carry orders from the brain to the heart, intestines, and lungs. Users walk a thin line as they increase the dosage.

Babies of women who took PCP while pregnant are easily startled, overreact to loud noises or sudden movements, and may be spastic, or display coarse tremors in their movements. Some will be born with Mongoloid features. Babies can also receive PCP through breast milk. If the drug is stopped, the infant will experience a severe withdrawal reaction.

PCP AND THE BRAIN

PCP does not affect the midbrain in the same way as cocaine. It does not cause the overproduction or underproduction of endorphins in the way the opiates affect that system. It does cause dopamine to remain in the released state in the same manner as cocaine and amphetamines. At the same time, increasing doses of PCP will interrupt the ability of the nerves to conduct messages: it becomes an anesthetic.

The anaesthetic action of PCP, the original use of the drug, can shut down pain receptors in the brain, and is the reason why people who have taken moderate doses will feel very little pain.

SOURCE NOTES

CHAPTER 1
1. Stephen Arterburn, "Cocaine and the Drug Epidemic," in *Growing Up Addicted: Why Our Children Abuse Alcohol and Drugs and What We Can Do About It* (New York: Ballantine, 1987), 257–272.
2. A. J. Giannini, M.D., "Phencyclidine," in *Drugs of Abuse,* ed. A. J. Giannini, M.D., and A. E. Slaby, M.D. (Oradell, N.J.: Medical Economics, 1989), 145–147.
3. Ruth R. Levine, *Pharmacology: Drug Actions and Reactions* (Boston: Little, Brown, 1978), 279.
4. Levine, *Pharmacology,* 341–366.
5. R. Bruck-Kan, *Introduction to Human Anatomy* (New York: Harper & Row, 1979), 446–447.

CHAPTER 2
1. The primary source of background information for this section is L. Grinspoon, M.D. and J. B. Bakalar, *Cocaine: A Drug and Its Social Evolution* (New York: Basic Books, 1985), 20–28.
2. Elixirs have been associated with cocaine abuse in the United States for over 100 years and have been the subject of many pharmacologic papers. See Grinspoon and Bakalar, "Cocaine," 22.
3. Ibid., 55–56.
4. Mark S. Gold, M.D., and A. J. Giannini, M.D., "Cocaine and Cocaine Addiction," in *Drugs of Abuse,* ed. A. J. Giannini,

M.D., and A. E. Slaby, M.D. (Oradell, N.J.: Medical Economics, 1989), 83–96.

5. Stephen Arterburn, "Cocaine and the Drug Epidemic," in *Growing Up Addicted: Why Our Children Abuse Alcohol and Drugs and What We Can Do About It* (New York: Ballantine, 1987), 257–272.

CHAPTER 3

1. Mark S. Gold, M.D., "Opiates," in *Drugs of Abuse,* ed. A. J. Giannini, M.D., and A. E. Slaby, M.D. (Oradell, N.J.: Medical Economics, 1989), 127–128.
2. Lawrence A. Young et al., *Recreational Drugs* (New York: Berkley, 1977) sections on opium, morphine, and heroin.
3. Kenneth J. Rose, *The Body in Time* (New York: John Wiley & Sons, 1988), 67.
4. Gold, "Opiates," 129–142.
5. Rose, *Body in Time,* 76.

CHAPTER 4

1. Aryeh L. Klahr, M.D., Herbert G. Roehrich, M.D., and Norman S. Miller, M.D., "Marijuana," in *Drugs of Abuse,* ed. A. J. Giannini, M.D., and A. E. Slaby, M.D. (Oradell, N.J.: Medical Economics, 1989), 97.
2. Ibid., 98–104.
3. Information on clinical depression exacerbated by drug abuse can be found in the following articles: "Depression: It Is Hitting Young Adults Harder than Ever Before," *Newsweek,* 4 May 1987, 48–55; "Panel Says Recurrent Mood Disorders Are Underdiagnosed, Undertreated," *Medical World News,* 31 May 1984, 17–18; F. Schumer, "Bye-Bye Blues: A New Wonder Drug for Depression," *New York Magazine,* 18 December 1989, 46–53; P. H. Wender, M.D., and D. F. Klein, M.D., "The Promise of Biological Psychiatry," *Psychology Today,* February 1981, 25–41.
4. Klahr, Roehrich, and Miller, "Marijuana," 98–104.
5. Ibid., 99.
6. Ibid., 104–122.
7. Ibid., 101.
8. For a highly technical discussion of the neuropharmacology of cannabis addiction, see Klahr, Roehrich and Miller, "Marijuana," 106–107: "Marijuana may be altering and redirecting the instincts; in a sense the marijuana has overtaken and is orchestrating the drive states. Dopamine, gamma-aminobutyric acid (GABA), serotonin, norepinephrine, and the

opioids [beta-endorphins] may undergo alteration in synaptic functions to enhance or diminish neurochemically the behavioral changes resulting from addiction."

9. Ibid., 107–113.
10. Ibid., 108, 120.
11. Geigy Pharmaceutical Laboratories, personal communication, 1988.

CHAPTER 5
1. R. Moreines, M.D., "The Psychedelics," in *Drugs of Abuse*, ed. A. J. Giannini, M.D., and A. E. Slaby, M.D. (Oradell, N.J.: Medical Economics, 1989) 207–216.
2. Kenneth J. Rose, *The Body in Time* (New York: John Wiley & Sons, 1988), 67–68.
3. Moreines, "Psychedelics," 217–239.
4. Rose, *Body in Time,* 76.
5. M. Teitler et al., "Receptor Pharmacology of MDMA and Related Hallucinogens," in *The Neuropharmacology of Serotonin,* ed. Patricia M. Whitaker-Azmitia and Stephen J. Peroutka, Annals of the New York Academy of Sciences, vol. 600 (Oct. 15, 1990), 626–637.

CHAPTER 6
1. Ruth R. Levine, *Pharmacology: Drug Actions and Reactions* (Boston: Little, Brown, 1978), 359–361.
2. N. S. Miller, M.D., and M. S. Gold, M.D., "Amphetamine and Its Derivatives," in *Drugs of Abuse,* ed. A. J. Giannini, M.D., and A. E. Slaby, M.D. (Oradell, N.J.: Medical Economics, 1989), 15–28.
3. Ibid., 29–40.

CHAPTER 7
1. A. J. Giannini, M.D., "Phencyclidine," in *Drugs of Abuse,* ed. A. J. Giannini, M.D., and A. E. Slaby, M.D. (Oradell, N.J.: Medical Economics, 1989), 145–147.
2. Ibid., 147–154.

GLOSSARY

Abuse drug: *See* **Drug abuse**.

Acquired Immune Deficiency Syndrome (AIDS): A group of diseases (syndrome) that develop as a result of the long-term effects of Human Immunodeficiency Virus (HIV infection) and can be seen anywhere from a few months to ten years after infection. HIV infects immune system cells. When HIV disease progresses to AIDS, the immune system cells that protect the body die in large numbers, and the body loses its ability to defend itself against any infection.

Addict: A person who has established a high tolerance and dependence upon a drug and needs to keep taking it to maintain what he or she perceives as a "normal" experience, and to stave off the physical and psychological effects of withdrawal.

Adrenal glands [uh-*dreen*-ul]: Located above the kidneys, the adrenal glands produce epinephrine (adrenaline), a hormone that increases heart rate as well as blood flow to the skeletal muscles, and causes the supply of additional fuel by the body's own storehouse (liver, fat cells).

Alkaloid [*al*-kah-loyd]: Naturally occurring substances produced by plants (cocaine, quinine) that have specific effects on the body.

Alveoli [al-*vee*-oh-lye]: Tiny sacs lining the lungs that remove carbon dioxide from the blood and provide oxygen to red blood cells, which circulate throughout the body. The alveoli have thin walls surrounded by capillaries where the transfer of gases to and from the blood takes place. Other molecules of gases and vapors can also pass through alveolar walls.

Amphetamine psychosis: A severe emotional disorder with symptoms similar to schizophrenia that include derangement of the personality, loss of contact with reality, paranoid delusions, and auditory hallucinations.

Amphetamines [am-*fet*-uh-meens]: A group of synthetic drugs that act on the central nervous system, increase the activity of the brain, and cause the release of epinephrine (adrenaline).

Anaphylactic shock [*an*-uh-fuh-*lak*-tik]: A type of shock caused by allergic reaction to a drug, insect sting, or certain foods. It involves several stages: swelling and hives; constriction of the blood vessels in the arms, legs, hands, and feet; sweating, high temperature, and runny nose; tightening in the chest; constriction of the trachea (preventing air from reaching the lungs), suffocation, and death.

Anesthetic [an-ehs-*thet*-ik]: Drug that makes the nerves in a small area or the entire body become numb to pain. An anesthetic works by dissolving in the insulating fatty tissue along nerves that permits transmission of impulses, and reverses their ability to conduct an electrical signal for a period of time. (This insulating tissue, called the myelin sheath, performs a function similar to the insulation around an electrical wire.)

Antidotes [*an*-tih-doats]: Drugs that are able to reverse harmful effects of other drugs or compounds. They can save a person's life, but cannot be given until the harmful drug is identified.

Aphrodisiac [af-ruh-*dee*-zee-ak]: A sexual stimulant.

Ataxia [uh-*tak*-see-uh]: An interruption of messages traveling through nerves that control the muscles of coordinated movement. Some muscles will move as they should. Others will start a movement that is not related.

Bhang: A liquid made by brewing the leaves of marijuana plants, used by priests in India for religious ceremonies in about 2000 B.C.

Brain hemorrhage [*hem*-eh-ridge]: The bursting of a blood vessel in the brain, releasing blood into the surrounding tissues.

Bronchi/Bronchioles [*bron*-kye/*bron*-kee-olz]: The wide and narrow tubes that lead from the trachea (in the throat) to the lungs.

Bronchitis [bron-*kite*-us]: A serious infection of the upper respiratory system.

Caffeine [ka-*feen*]: A mild stimulant found in coffee, tea, and cola drinks.

Cannabis [*kan*-ah-biss]: (*Cannabis sativa*) The more commonly used scientific name for marijuana, a plant that contains 421 known chemicals, including the intoxicating, psychoactive drug, delta-9-THC.

Cardiovascular system [kard-ee-oh-*vas*-kyuh-luhr]: All of the arteries, arterioles, veins, venules [veen-ules], and capillaries in the body. The smallest vessels, the capillaries, surround groups of cells in the organs and muscles, and are the structures where smaller arteries (arterioles) carrying blood from the lungs and heart meet smaller veins (venules) that carry blood to the heart and lungs.

Cataleptic reaction [*kat*-uhl-*ep*-tik]: A condition in which the body is held rigid while the individual is flushed and perspires heavily. In addition, the mind races through disorganized thoughts accompanied by irritability along with powerful euphoria, and, at times, visual hallucinations.

Central nervous system: The brain and the spinal cord.

Cerebellum: [ser-uh-*bel*-um]: The part of the brain that controls muscular coordination.

Cerebrovascular spasm [suh-*ree*-broh-*vas*-kyuh-luhr]: The blood vessels leading to the brain constrict. If this occurs for more than about 8 minutes, the entire brain dies of a lack of oxygen.

Cerebrum [suh-*ree*-brum]: The part of the brain that controls emotions, reactions to pain, pleasure, and judgment.

Chromosomes [*kro*-muh-soamz]: Genetic structures, found in every cell of the body, made of long chains of genes that carry the instructions for making all the compounds used to build and repair tissues.

Cilia [*sil*-ee-uh]: Tightly packed, microscopic, threadlike structures lining the bronchi. They beat in rhythmic waves to stop particles of dust from entering the lungs, and are the first line of defense for the respiratory system.

Coca [*koh*-kuh]: A plant that grows wild in South America, the leaves of which contain the alkaloid cocaine.

Convulsions: [kun-*vul*-shuns]: Abnormal violent and involuntary contractions of the muscles of the arms, legs, bladder, bowel, and diaphragm, the muscle used for breathing.

Cranial nerves [*kray*-nee-uhl]: Nerves that control the muscles and sensory organs of the cranium (skull).

Delirium [di-*lir*-ee-uhm]: A severely disordered and excited organic mental state that occurs very suddenly.

Dependence: The need to keep taking a drug regularly, either for its effects on the body (to curtail withdrawal symptoms) or its effects on the mind (to maintain a mental state, such as euphoria).

Depression [di-*presh*-un]: A feeling of extreme sadness that can develop into a disease of the emotions caused by very disappointing and frustrating experiences. It can lead to inactivity, difficulty in concentrating, and loss of appetite. Depression can also be an organic emotional disease that may not be related to causes in real life. People who suffer from organic depression cannot control it because certain chemicals in their brains are different from normal brain chemistry. Doctors have recently found new ways of treating this depression with compounds that stop the reactions in the brain that cause this deep sadness.

Designer drugs: A group of psychedelic hallucinogens created by attaching psychoactive chemicals to amphetamine molecules. Includes such mind-altering drugs as STP and Ecstasy.

Dissociatives [dis-*o*-she-*ate*-ivz]: Drugs that cause the powerful expression of only part of the personality, so that users lose a sense of who they are and behave violently.

Dopamine [*do*-pah-meen]: The neurotransmitter that controls feelings of pleasure.

Drug: Any isolated, purified chemical or natural substance that affects or alters physical performance, psychological motivations, or emotional behavior.

Drug abuse: Nonmedical use of drugs in ways that are neither sensible nor acceptable, and possibly harmful for the user as well as others. Dependence on the drug can lead to physical and mental deterioration.

Dysphoria [dis-*for*-ee-uh]: A feeling of impatience and restlessness combined with the feelings of sadness and anger.

Emphysema [emm-fi-*zee*-mah]: A disease in which the alveoli of the lungs fill with fluid, stretch, and form pockets that cannot be cleared, creating a condition that is similar to drowning.

Encopresis [en-koh-*pree*-sus]: The inability to control the release of feces.

Endocarditis [en-doe-car-*dy*-tiss]: An infection of the tissue that lines the heart.

Endorphins [en-*dor*-finz]: The body's natural painkillers that are produced in the midbrain and brain stem.

Epinephrine [ep-uh-*nef*-run]: The powerful hormone that plays an important role in the "flight or fight" reaction to danger, and is the body's antidote for histamine release in anaphylactic shock. Also called adrenaline.

Ergot: A fungus on rye and other grasses that produces an LSD-type hallucinogen.

Euphoria [you-*for*-ee-ah]: An exaggerated state of physical and emotional well-being.

Flashback: When a person has visions, hears sounds or voices, senses odd combinations of feelings on his skin, or experiences the same emotions he had when high on a psychedelic drug. Flashbacks are common in 25 percent of the people who have used psychedelic hallucinogens.

Glaucoma [glauh-*ko*-muh]: An eye disease in which increased pressure within the eye damages the retina, causing impaired vision and sometimes blindness.

Glomeruli [gluh-*mer*-uh-lye]: Specialized structures in the kidney that separate molecules to be returned to the body from urea that is added to urine.

Glycogen [*gly*-koh-jen]: Long chains of carbohydrate molecules (glucose) linked together by the liver for the purpose of storing fuel, that are converted back to short molecules when fuel is required by the body for any and all of its functions.

Hallucinations [huh-*loos*-un-*a*-shuns]: Images seen by the mind that do not exist in the real world.

Hallucinogens [huh-*loos*-un-uh-juhnz]: Psychoactive chemicals or drugs that induce hallucinations and cause changes in sensory perception and emotional reactions. See also *psychedelic hallucinogens*.

Hashish [*hash*-eesh]: Extracted from marijuana leaves and flowers by cooking the plant matter with water and evaporating the liquid until a paste remains.

Heart failure: Can be caused by obstruction, collapse, or bursting of the vessels that bring blood to the heart.

Hepatitis [*hep*-uh-*tyte*-us]: A viral infection of the liver.

Heroin [*hehr*-uh-win]: Chemically refined morphine.

Histamine [*hiss*-tuh-meen]: A chemical that stimulates the muscles of the stomach and intestines, causes blood vessels to dilate, and increases the flow of fluids. Also used by the body in healing processes, such as causing the flow of a clear liquid called lymph into a small cut, providing the necessary fluid for immune system cells and repair cells to pass through tissues and fight infection.

Hyperreflexia [hy-pur-ree-*flecks*-ee-uh]: An above-normal increase in the speed of muscular reflexes.

Hypertension [hy-pur-*ten*-chun]: High blood pressure.

Hyperthermia [hy-pur-*thur*-mee-uh]: Very high fever.

Hyperthyroidism [hy-pur-*thy*-royd-iz-um]: A condition caused by an overactivity of the thyroid gland. Symptoms include weight loss, restlessness, bulging of the eyes, and sometimes goiter (enlargement of the thyroid gland).

Hyporeflexia [hy-poh-ree-*flecks*-ee-uh]: When the reflexes of the body are decreased in intensity.

Hypothalamus [hy-poh-*thal*-uh-muss]: An area of the midbrain, located near the underside of the brain and above the pituitary gland, that includes among its functions production of vasopressin, a hormone that enhances the performance of human memory and controls blood pressure by causing the kidneys to return as much water to the body as possible.

Illegal drug: A drug that has been identified as a substance that can cause bodily harm, or addiction, or both, and is associated with organized crime.

Inert substances: [in-*urf*]: Nonreactive substances.

Kidneys: Organs that remove waste products from the body (such as urea) to form a solution called urine that is excreted by the bladder.

Limbic system: The area of the brain containing the reward system, which controls moods and reactions that ensure personal survival and may be the location for specific chemical pathways of THC addiction.

Liver: The organ that removes poisons, manufactures molecules necessary for important processes, and stores fuel in the form of glycogen.

Locus ceruleus [*loh*-kus seh-*roo*-lee-us]: An area of the brain that contains many endorphin receptors and controls reactions to pain and pleasure.

LSD: d-Lysergic acid diethylamide, [*dee*-lie-*surr*-jik *ass*-id dye-ethel-*amm*-eyed]: A psychedelic hallucinogen that may be man-made (synthetic) or refined from rye seed ergot (a fungus that produces the drug in its raw form).

Lung cancer: A disease in which cells in the lung stop growing normally, multiply wildly, and no longer carry out the process of breathing.

Macrophages [*mak*-ruh-faj-ez]: The cells that trigger the immune response, which causes other cells to manufacture antibodies and attack invading organisms in groups. These cells also clear away dead tissues.

Mannitol [*man*-ih-tall]: A weak laxative used to "cut," or dilute, cocaine.

Medulla [meh-*doo*-lah]: A structure located where the spinal cord enters the brain; controls respiration, blood pressure, heart rate, and vomiting.

Meningitis [men-in-*jy*-tiss]: An infection of the meninges, a layer of tissue that surrounds the central nervous system (the brain and spinal cord).

Mescaline [*mes*-kuh-leen]: A psychedelic hallucinogen produced from the buttons (buds) of the peyote cactus found in the southwestern United States and Central America.

Metabolized [muh-*tab*-uh-lyzed]: Subject to metabolism, the process by which substances are broken down in the body to be used for energy.

Methadone [*meh*-thuh-doan]: A legal substitute for heroin, used to gradually free an addict from the drug.

Midbrain: The area of the brain that includes the hypothalamus, the thalamus, and the locus ceruleus.

Morphine [*mor*-feen]: A chemically refined product of opium that is used to make heroin.

Mutagen [*myout*-uh-jen]: A compound, chemical, or drug that causes mutations, or irregular changes, in the genetic material of cells.

Myoclonus [mye-oh-*kloh*-nuss]: A spasmodic jerking of muscles.

Narcolepsy [*nahr*-kuh-lep-see]: A condition characterized by attacks of deep sleep.

Narcotic analgesic [nar-*kaht*-ic an-nill-*jee*-zik]: A stupor-producing drug (narcotic) that stops pain (analgesic).

Neurotransmitters [noor-oh-tranz-*mit*-erz]: Chemicals that carry impulses from one nerve cell to another across a synapse.

Nystagmus [nis-*tag*-muhs]: Involuntary and repetitive rapid movement of the eyeballs from side to side.

Opiate [*oh*-pee-ehtt]: Drug made from opium.

Opioids [*oh*-pee-oydz]: Original name for endorphins (see separate entry).

Opisthotonos [oh-pis-thot-*o*-nuss]: The head and legs are pulled back by sudden clenching of back muscles, causing the body to arch forward.

Opium [*oh*-pee-uhm]: The raw, pasty product of the opium poppy produced by boiling the flowers with water and evaporating the fluid.

Paranoia [paar-uh-*noy*-uh]: An intense feeling of fear that does not have a basis in reality and very often comes from being afraid of something in oneself, such as anger.

Paregoric [par-uh-*gor*-ik]: A solution of opium mixed with camphor. Camphor is the same compound that is used in moth balls.

Paresthesia [par-us-*thee*-zhuh]: A combination of feelings on the skin such as burning, shivering, crawling, caused by a drug.

Peristalsis [per-uh-*stall*-sus]: The process that moves food from one stage of the digestive system to the next through contraction of the muscular walls of the stomach and intestines.

Peyote [pay-*oht*-ee]: The milk squeezed out of cactus buttons (buds) that contain mescaline, a psychedelic hallucinogen.

Pharmacology [far-muh-*kahl*-uh-gee]: The study of drugs and how they affect the body.

Phencyclidine (PCP) [fen-*sik*-luh-*deen*]: One of the dissociatives, a class of mind-altering drugs with effects similar to those caused by the sympathomimetics and psychedelic hallucinogens. PCP is a central nervous system depressant and anesthetic that is legally used to quiet laboratory animals for experiments. It is illegally used for its effects as a depressant or stimulant and as a substitute for other illegal drugs, and is known to cause violent rage reactions. More commonly known as angel dust.

Piloerection [py-loh-ee-*reck*-shun]: The hair stands on end.

Pneumonia [noo-*moan*-ya]: An often curable disease in which the lungs become infected and fill with fluid.

Pons [pahnz]: From the Latin meaning "bridge." The structure that joins the spinal cord with the mass of the brain, just after the medulla.

Psilocybin [*sih*-luh-*sye*-buhn]: A psychedelic extract from the psilocybe family of mushrooms. Also known as magic mushroom.

Psychedelic [*sye*-ku-*del*-ik]: Mind-altering.

Psychedelic hallucinogens: Potent drugs that change the way the brain perceives (understands), as well as the way thoughts and feelings are produced, and have the ability to make the user see, hear, and feel complete experiences that are happening only in the mind. Also known as psychedelics.

Psychoactive: Affecting the mind or behavior.

Psychopharmacology [*si*-ko-far-muh-*kahl*-uh-gee]: The study of the effects of drugs on behavior and personality.

Psychosis [sy-*ko*-sus]: A type of mental illness that causes people to lose the ability to meet the normal demands of life, such as studying or going to work. Characterized by extremely disturbed behavior and a total break with reality: becoming lost in oneself, drifting away from family, friends, and surrounding occurrences.

Psychotic [sy-*kot*-ik]: A person or mental state characterized by behavior demonstrating a total break with reality.

Quinine [*kwy*-nyne]: An alkaloid from the bark of the cinchona tree of South America, used to treat malaria and stomach ailments. It is also used to dilute cocaine.

Reefer: The name for a marijuana cigarette, coined by sailors in the 1920s. It comes from "reefing a sail," the process of rolling up a sail during a storm so that less sail area will be exposed to a strong wind.

Reflex: A reflex consists of an action and a reaction. If the action is touching a hot stove (stimulus), the reaction consists of sensory nerves carrying the message of intense heat to the spinal cord and brain as pain, and the message or response sent by the brain and the spinal cord to the motor nerves that tell the muscles to pull the hand away.

Respiration: The transfer of carbon dioxide from the bloodstream to the lungs, and the transfer of oxygen from the lungs to the bloodstream.

Respiratory System: The system of the body that processes oxygen and removes carbon dioxide. The upper respiratory system consists of the tubes that conduct air into the lungs. It begins with the trachea, located in the neck, and leads to two larger tubes in the lungs, called the bronchi, lined with microscopic, muscular, threadlike structures, called cilia, which beat in rhythmic waves. These stop particles of dust from entering the lungs, and are the first line of defense for the respiratory system. The lower respiratory system consists of smaller tubes in the lungs, called bronchioles, that lead to the alveoli (see separate entry), together with the lobes of the lungs, the connective tissues that house the respiratory system.

Reticular formation [rheh-*tik*-yu-lahr]: Those tissues in the brain that take shape after the medulla, extend through the pons, spread out to all the areas of the brain, and are responsible for normal wakefulness and alertness.

Rhinitis [ry-*ny*-tiss]: Infection of the nose.

Schizophrenia [skit-suh-*fre*-ne-uh]: A type of mental illness that begins after adolescence or in young adulthood. This illness causes inability to understand concepts about the world (such as "people are to be respected, not killed"), as well as disturbances in behavior and in thought process. Indicators of this illness are withdrawing from reality, confused or abusive responses to people, mood swings, and childlike thoughts about adult problems, often accompanied by hallucinations.

Serotonin [sir-uh-*toh*-nun]: The neurotransmitter that controls the feeling of being satisfied after eating or other experiences that cause pleasure.

Sinusitis [sye-nuh-*seyet*-us]: Infection of the sinuses.

Speed: A street name for amphetamines, usually used to refer to amphetamine sulfate, a mixture of equal amounts of levoamphetamine and dextroamphetamine. Other names include pep pills, crank, crystal, meth, go, go fast, zip, uppers, bennies, and chris.

Speedballs: A very potent, addictive combination of heroin and cocaine.

Stereotopy [*ster*-ee-uh-*ty*-pee]: An uncontrollable need to repeat the same movement, such as picking up a cup from a table and placing it on another table, back and forth, until the need wears off.

Stimulant: A drug that causes the release of epinephrine (see separate entry) and affects the central nervous system, especially the brain, which responds with feelings of intense alertness, increased physical and mental strength, and eliminates (or severely decreases) feelings of tiredness, hunger and pain. A weak stimulant is the caffeine in tea and coffee. Amphetamines are far more powerful.

Stroke: The blockage and/or bursting of a blood vessel in an area of the brain followed by collapse of nearby blood vessels.

Strychnine [*strik*-nyne]: A deadly poison that, in very small doses, will cause mild tachycardia. Convulsions accompany a slightly greater dose, and death in a matter of minutes follows a moderate dose.

Sympathetic nervous system: Part of the autonomic, or involuntary, nervous system. A chain of spinal nerves whose functions include contraction of blood vessels, increase of heart rate, and regulation of glandular secretions.

Sympathomimetic [*sim*-puh-thoh-muh-*met*-ik]: Chemical changes in the brain, caused by a drug; they mimic or copy the normal chemical reactions that engage the sympathetic division of the nervous system.

Synapse [*sin*-aapss]: The gap between nerve endings that is crossed by neurotransmitters to carry impulses from one nerve to another throughout the nervous system.

Tachycardia [taa-ki-*car*-dee-ya]: A rapid heart beat.

Thalamus [*thal*-uh-muss]: A part of the midbrain responsible for interpreting pain.

THC (tetrahydrocannabinoids): [*tet*-rah-high-drow-kan-*naa*-bih-noydz]: The intoxicating drugs in marijuana, the most powerful of which is the psychoactive delta-9-THC.

Tolerance: When the body becomes accustomed to a drug, so that the initial dose has less of an effect, and increasing doses must be taken to achieve the desired effect.

Toxic [*tocks*-ik]: Poisonous.

Trachea [*tray*-kee-uh]: Also known as the windpipe, part of the upper respiratory system that conducts air into the lungs, and is located before the bronchi [*brahn*-kigh].

Tremor [*trem*-uhr]: An involuntary trembling or shaking, most noticeable in the hands.

Withdrawal: The unpleasant effects on the body and mind caused by suddenly discontinuing an addictive drug after becoming dependent on it.

FOR FURTHER READING

AMPHETAMINES

Edelson, Edward. *Drugs and the Brain*. New York: Chelsea House, 1987.

Grinspoon, Lester. *The Speed Culture: Amphetamine Use and Abuse in America*. Cambridge, Mass.; Harvard University Press, 1975.

CANNABIS, HEROIN, AND PHENCYCLIDINE (PCP)

Johnston, L.D., O'Malley, P.M., and Bachman, J.G. *Use of Licit and Illicit Drugs by America's High School Students, 1975–1984*. Rockville, Md.: National Institute of Drug Abuse, 1985.

McCormick, Michele. *Designer-Drug Abuse*. New York: Franklin Watts, 1989.

Russell, George K. *Marihuana Today*. New York: The Myrin Institute for Adult Education, 1980.

United States Department of Health and Human Services. *Etiology of Drug Abuse: Implications for Prevention*. Washington, D.C.: General Printing Office, 1985. (Etiology means the causes or reasons for an occurrence.)

COCAINE

Boundy, D. and Washton, A. *Cocaine and Crack*. Hillside, N.J.: Enslow Publishers, 1989.

Grinspoon, L. and Backalar, J.B. *Cocaine: A Drug and Its Social Evolution*. New York: Basic Books, 1985.

Johanson, Chris-Ellyn. *Cocaine: A New Epidemic*. New York: Chelsea House, 1986.

HALLUCINOGENS

Miller, Mark S. *Bad Trips*. New York: Chelsea House, 1988.

Snyder, Solomon. *Drugs and the Brain*. New York: Scientific American Books, 1989.

INDEX

143